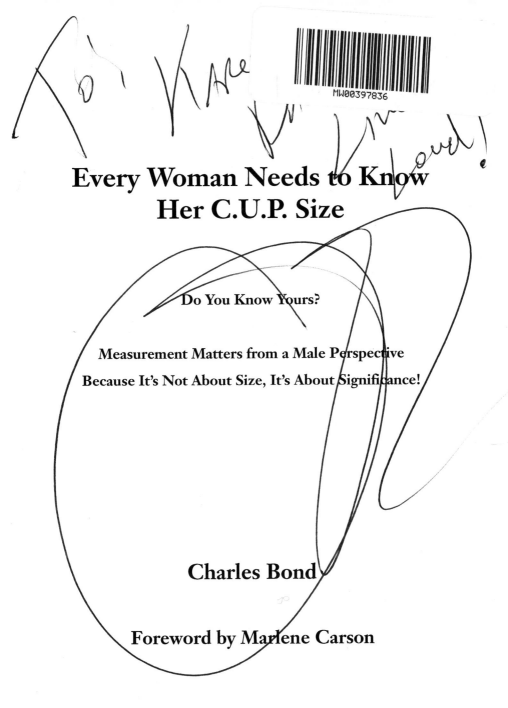

Every Woman Needs to Know Her C.U.P. Size

Do You Know Yours?

Measurement Matters from a Male Perspective

Because It's Not About Size, It's About Significance!

Charles Bond

Foreword by Marlene Carson

First published by Dog Ear Publishing
4011 Vincennes Road
Indianapolis, IN 46268
www.dogearpublishing.net

ISBN: 978-0-9860-7320-5

Library of Congress Control Number: has been applied for

This book is printed on acid-free paper.

Printed in the United States of America

Unless otherwise indicated, scripture quotations are taken from the King James Version of the Bible. Copyright © 1979, 1980, 1982 by Thomas Nelson, Inc. All Rights Reserved

Scripture quotations marked NIV are taken from The Holy Bible, New International Version, © 1973, 1978, 1984, 2011 All Rights reserved

Scripture quotations marked MSG are taken from The Message by Eugene Peterson © 1993, 1994, 1995, 1996, 2000, 2001, 2002. All rights reserved.

Short Story quotations throughout Cup Size Matters by Author John Mason, Pastor Tolan Morgan, Pastor Bertrand Bailey, Dr. Cindy Trimm, and Bishop TD Jakes.

Acknowledgments

To my Lord and Savior Jesus Christ—somehow words fail, when I attempt to convey my appreciation for all you've done. My destiny is within your mind, my call is within your heart, and my purpose is within your hand. I am persuaded that nothing will separate me from you!

To my parents, Charles Edward Bond Sr. and Shirley Lee Hill Bond, you're a rare commodity in these times. You provided safety, encouragement, and support. Before I knew God, I knew you. Thank you for being there.

To Ruka Mae (Honey) Bond, my paternal grandmother and Margeree "Madea" Robertson, my maternal grandmother; gone but never forgotten. Without you there would be no me!

Mama Nettie, I still have the key to your house.

To my siblings…you've invested so much in me. Sharon Williams, Gwendolyn Clark and Brendolyn Paige—you three exemplify what real sisters are. In your own way, each of you helped to mother and nurture me. Thank you! McKinley Britton—my brother—your strength has made me a prisoner of hope. To my brother Anthony (Tony) Britton (posthumously) gone but never forgotten may you rest in Heaven.

To the greatest Church in the world, New Wine Church International— You are not my bride, because you are the bride of Christ; you are not my body, because you are the body of Christ; but you are my backbone. You have been there every step of the way and I want to thank you for being an Obedient Church who sowed into me and my life. Because of you, "WE" now touch the entire planet. (We are living out our mission, because our works speak louder than our words).

To the great men who served as an influence upon my life; not only in word but in deed. Your actions speak volumes; and your words speak wisdom. Dr. Frank E. Ray, Sr. you are a jewel; there is salt between us. Bishop Ed Stephens you spoke life into me when death crouched at my door. Bishop T.D. Jakes you blazed the trail with *Woman Thou Art Loosed.* Mr. Steve Harvey, your literary work, *"Act Like A Lady, Think like a Man"* has been an inspiration.

To my (bestie) Kristen Yates, Harry and Elizabeth Scotts grand daughter, what can I say? Saints

To Ms. Marlene Carson, for making me tap into this big head of mine and realize that if I can talk about it, I can write about it. Without your belief in the vision for this movement, women all over the world would still be guessing their cup size and asking the age-old question "...am I here for...?" You rock girlfriend!

Lastly, to all the beautiful women in the world who don't curse your curves or damn your design. You bear in your breast LIFE; and that life abundantly. Please remember this book is not about SIZE...it's about SIGNIFICANCE.

Now Let's Build a C.U.P. Size World, every woman on the planet needs to know her C.U.P. Size!

Charles Bond / Life Coach

Contents

Foreword

**"So God created man in his own image, in the image of God
created he him; male and female created he them"** (Genesis 1:27).

Who is woman? Societal and cultural norms have defined her many ways, causing her to be ruled, subjugated, abused, and distrusted. She has been grounded both emotionally and spiritually into a dry dust that falls short of the Lord's invested purpose for her role within humanity. We know that God fashioned a perfect creation, then shared His instruction for life, replete with both joy and purpose. However, it seems that we must now refashion the thinking and self-image of even the most God-fearing woman, so that she may effectively stand firm in a Godly knowledge of who (and whose) she is. Therefore, we must gather the dry dust and pour into her the water of the Word, so that she will become a moldable clay—fashioned into spiritual vessels for the Lord's use—solidified by truth.

In Every Woman Needs to Know Her C.U.P. Size Charles E. Bond teaches us that, "Knowing is doing!" From his perspective, one could claim knowledge of things great and small; but it was only when knowledge is demonstrated that he has an assurance that one truly gained knowledge of what was being taught. Knowing truly is doing, for it is the possession of truth that catalyzes change, empowers one to dispel falsehoods, and encourages the declaration of personal freedoms. In one's life travels, oftentimes it is truth of one's self that is most deeply hidden. The search for one's self, for many, is a lifetime journey. Who am I? What is God's plan for me? What is my purpose? These basic questions remain part of the very foundation of our worldview; shaping how we perceive ourselves as individuals, our lives and its content, and the world in which we live.

In this prolific writing *Bond* illuminates our thinking—bringing about awareness that, at the time of creation, no aspect of mankind was outside of God's purview and design. "...male and female created He them" (Genesis 1:27b). The fullness of mankind, perfect in his design and purpose, was within him at the point of his fashioning by God's own hand. Male and female—a singular unit with individual and collective Calling, Uniqueness, and Purpose; there was no afterthought called woman. Mankind—both male and female—was called Adam and within his cellular makeup was the investment of dominion power, authority, and spiritual impetus to fulfill the will and commandments of God.

While cultural and religious teachings seek to suppress the spiritual positioning and authority of women, it is through embracing the truth of God's Word that she gains the wherewithal to walk out the fullness of her role within humanity; whether as wife and mother or as a fellow servant in the vineyard. There is a clarion call to embrace Godly purpose—not usurping authority, but regaining God-ordained position of bone of his bone and flesh of his flesh, firm in all aspects of Biblical holiness and Godliness.

As you begin to develop your answers to those familiar questions "Who am I?", "What is God's plan for me?", and "What is my purpose?" remember, knowing is doing. That means that the pursuit of God, His truth, and His purpose may require that you lay aside your self-perceptions, your individual plans and dreams, and whole-heartedly chase God with reckless abandon. *Bond* brings us a call to action along this journey. Knowing is doing; and there are some things that every woman needs to know, her CUP Size that is. Maintaining the understanding that it is not about size but it's about significance.

Marlene Carson, Founder Rahabs Hideaway

Cup size Praise!

Every Woman Needs to Know Her C.U.P. Size is simply captivating! Charles Bond sketches an alternative route for ensuring that every woman on the planet knows her C.U.P. size! This book makes such impressive sense, that its distinctive style of explaining calling, uniqueness and purpose will provoke both thought and emotion! Empowering women across the world to walk in their destiny that God has for them. As an avid reader, this will be a go-to book for many years to come!
~Alisha C. Hill, Howard University

Powerful, hilarious and thought-provoking...this book creates an irresistible urge to become our best self. Charles Bond is a remarkable voice whose gift for narrative and wit offers a compassionate perspective on empowering women just where they find themselves.

Our private conversations are finally getting a public response, one that inspires deep belly laughter and unexpected tears from finding some part of ourselves in these pages. It is certain that from the discovery of our C.U.P. size, that no one will leave this book unchanged!
~Dr. Jothany Blackwood/ Dean of Fine,Performing, and Communications Arts, Fresno City College

Every generation has its Moses; you know the leader that moves people from a place of stagnation and complacency to a place of destiny. In past generations that leader may have sparked a flame that became the foundation and begun a movement that set the precedence for how we live for years to come. A few of those greats have names that are etched in the faith hall of fame like , Kenneth Hagin who launched Rhema Bible College , or Oral Roberts who launched ORU , and now this generation has its Moses with the release of Cup Size Matters. Charles Bond name has been carved into the hallowed halls of purpose and faith with this great book. This book challenges the reader to take an introspective look and realize that their calling uniqueness and purpose matters the most. It is a page turner as the information is dropped in the heart with each word on every page. Every woman needs every word in all twelve chapters of this book.

~Elder Tamra T. Eddy Author

Knowledge is power... and once a woman understands, embraces and celebrates her own C.U.P size...she can move freely with comfort and ease, being her best self, ON purpose, WITH purpose!!
~Shirley Murdock / Singer Songwriter

Every Woman Needs to Know Her C.U.P. Size touches every fiber of a woman who is on a journey to wholeness and freedom in Christ. Bishop Bond goes where no man has gone in a book...to make sure women walk upright in their calling, uniqueness, and purpose. He starts and finishes the conversation that every woman should have had long ago with your father, brother, uncle...about yourself.
~Lori Peterson Minister New Wine Church International

"Riveting, risque' and unrivaled, "Every Woman Needs to Know Her C.U.P. Size", compels women from all walks of life to confidently pursue, promote and position themselves to walk into their God ordained purpose. Its provocative nature, play on words and humor laced language provokes interest for readers as its message manages the heart and soul of the matter. Charles Bond, one of the most profound voices of our time, has penned a literary work that shall shake, save and settle men and women for generations to come."
~Michelle Pringle, Commercial Freelance Writer and Editor

In Charles Bond's book Every Woman Should Know their Cup Size is definitely a life-changing read. He makes himself completely relatable to women, and he reaches the soul of a person, but also challenges the readers to look into themselves in away that is healing, but also inspiring. I enjoyed seeing how he challenges the mind of the reader to think bigger, and deeper into their concepts of thought and perspective. This book is definitely going to change the world from the very first chapter he shows you that this is not a filler buster book, but that his insight and writing is truly given by God.

The wisdom that Charles relays is truly empowering. I believe that this book can change any woman of any age. It is very well written and needed. I believe that it's right on target with women needing to recognize the true potential in their purpose. I believe that it is a manual for women who are looking for how to reach their destiny and overcome obstacles of life.

I think Charles perspective is fresh and modern and it makes his demographic of women that much easier to get to which is not easy with him being a man. This is absolutely empowering for the right now generation fighting to understand their ultimate position and purpose in Christ.

As a woman, wife, mother, and daughter of Bishop Jakes and First Lady Jakes walking in purpose is something that I relate to very well, and also encourage women and men to do. I can say direction in getting to your purpose and destiny is something that we can all grasp a little bit of guidance and wisdom in, and Charles is giving that direction, guidance, and wisdom. The art of his message is going to change the world. I'm blessed to be part of such a wonderful movement and powerful message.

~Cora Jakes Coleman – Daughter of Bishop T.D. Jakes
and Lady Serita Jakes

"Every woman needs to do herself a favor and read this book. It is absolutely refreshing to gain a man's perspective on the invaluable worth of a woman! I will be incorporating some of these teachings into The Classy Lady Ministry."

~Crystal Janine Walton

"The author's straightforward prose captures the essence and tenacity of a woman. "Every Woman Needs to Know Her C.U.P Size" is a memorable, inspiring and life changing book. Its breadth and scope, the variety of data explored, and the stark nature of the argument will provoke both thought and emotion. Every woman should explore her true C.U.P. size, is an affirming message and is a must read..... a gem to be treasured."

~Janeé Jenkins, Executive Director/Founder
Of X-Clusive Empowerment Network For Women

Never before has the proper empowerment of women in the church been more critical. Charles Bond is genius... It's all in their C.U.P. Size!

~Windie Lazenko, Founder and CEO, 4H.E.R. North Dakota

As a survivor of human trafficking I have struggle for years trying to identify and find the missing pieces of my life; now I know it's in my C.U.P. size. Thank you Charles Bond…What a reality to know it's not about size but significance.

~Survivor Elesondra DeRomano

"*Every Woman Needs to Know Her C. U. P. Size* is a must read for all women. Charles drives home the message that women have true value and can live life on purpose. It is a life guide that women should keep within reach so that they can return to the book and read again and again."

~DeLores Pressley, Founder, The Up Woman Network

CHAPTER 1

God Couldn't Have Been a Woman ... Or Could He?

Have you ever wondered what was God thinking? I mean, honestly, all that women have to endure—from menstrual cycles to makeup, God couldn't have been a woman. Or that age old question of whether God was male or female. This question has caused many fights, conflicts, and possibly even wars. The whole concept of God is a conundrum; therefore, the gender of the Creator of all humankind is the question that begs attention, only second to whether or not God exists. Well, I'm not here to argue that question because I stand on two very clear and concise axioms.

First, any god that needs to be proven is no god at all; so, yes, there is absolutely, positively, and unequivocally God. I'll venture further to say that there is only one true and living God. But because this is not necessarily a book on religion, I'll stick to the subject matter.

Secondly, although this is not a book about beliefs, let me say that God is a spirit, and those who worship Him must worship Him in spirit and in truth, so gender in the spiritual realm is not as big of an issue as we make it in the physical realm. However, I believe the only way to answer this age-old question is to read the only book that God ever wrote. Because, in a generation where we love absolutes and love to make an issue out of anything and everything—from why was the Olympic Gold medalist Gabby Douglas' hair done the way it was to whether it was okay for Miley Cyrus to twerk on national television, to whether or not it was okay for Phil Robertson (the father of the now-famous Robertson family) on A&E's *Duck Dynasty* to exercise his freedom of speech. Whatever the case, I don't think that we need to be overly sensitive or argumentative about God's gender as much as we need to focus on being what He created us to be. God has placed in the woman a plethora of gifts and abilities that fuel the engine of all humanity. So, it is my prayer that you are able to discover your CUP size, because it's really not about size, it's about significance. God's gender is irrelevant in the grander scheme of things, because if you were able to prove it, what would it do besides give you bragging rights, right? Wrong! No, it would serve as a source of information, but not change your circumstance or situation. God is God, point-blank, and God is a Spirit. But whatever the case, He deposited a little bit of Himself into all of us, regardless of gender, race, age, and so on. I heard one writer declare that we are referred to as masterpieces because we are all pieces of the Master.

> [14] Thank you for making me so wonderfully complex! It is amazing to think about. Your workmanship is marvelous—and how well I know it.

> —Psalm 139:14 (TLB)

I'm Normally Not Easily Impressed

I must admit, it normally takes a lot to impress me, yet I've always been impressed with the way God made us: one-third iron, one-quarter sulfur, 53 percent water, 11 percent hydrogen, 253 bones, 978 miles of blood vessels, and 608 muscles. I've always been impressed with the way God made man. He gave us two eyes that flash like cameras, every time they blink they take a picture and send it to the brain to be developed. He gave man thirty-two teeth in his mouth and thirty-seven feet of intestines. Man has four hundred cups in his tongue to differentiate the difference between sweet and sour. The brain of a man averages three pounds and two ounces, and the brain of a woman averages two pounds and eleven ounces. He gave man two hands; each hand has twenty-seven bones and thirty-nine muscles. The twenty-seven bones represent the twenty-seven books of the New Testament, and the thirty-nine muscles represent the thirty-nine books of the Old Testament. Then He turned around and told us what to do with each part of the body.

With our hands, He gave us Ecclesiastes 9:10, which says, "Whatsoever thy hand findeth to do, do *it* with thy might; for *there is* no work, nor device, nor knowledge, nor wisdom, in the grave, whither thou goest."

With our eyes, He gave us Psalms 121:1, "I will lift up mine eyes unto the hills, from whence cometh my help."

With our knees, He gave us Philippians 2:10, which says, "At the name of Jesus every knee should bow, of *things* in heaven, and *things* in earth, and *things* under the earth."

With our mouths, He gave us Philippians 2:11 (KJV), which says, "*That* every tongue should confess that Jesus Christ *is* Lord, to the glory of God the Father."

With our feet, He gave us Hebrews 12:1, which says, "Wherefore seeing we also are compassed about with so great a cloud of witnesses, let us lay aside every weight, and the sin which doth so easily beset *us*, and let us *run* with patience the race that is set before us."

With our minds, He gave us Philippians 2:5 (KJV), which says, "Let this mind be in you, which was also in Christ Jesus."

With the rest of our bodies, He gave us Romans 12:1, which says,

"I beseech you therefore, brethren, by the mercies of God, that ye present your bodies a living sacrifice, holy, acceptable unto God, *which is* your reasonable service."

He not only made us, but He told us what to do with every part of the body. God made us wonderfully, which means "full of wonder." The body is a built-in, self-contained hospital if maintained properly. Yet, the most impressive thing about our bodies is that God made them and then entrusted us to manage them. Take better care of your earth suit. It's the only one you've got. And the way to start as a woman who will live out loud is by knowing your CUP size. Watch what you put inside your body. It was meant to wear, not be a wastebasket. God is so wise that in all of His sovereignty, He knew then as He knows now what He desires for that which He designed. So, God's gender is not as important as us knowing why He designed us with gender. I believe that both male and female represent the masculine and feminine sides of God's nature; therefore, we represent the fullest extent of having the crown glory of His resemblance in human form. God couldn't have been a woman! Or could He?

Whether or not this is the case is something I will leave for those who have time to fight it out. I am too busy living in my purpose to try to figure out what the Almighty has already worked out. I just celebrate you because when I look at my fellow man and woman, I see one race—the human race—and I also see pieces of the Creator, and for that reason, I choose to be kind, gentle, caring, and loving to my fellow man and woman. When we realize this coupled with the fact that we are more alike than different, war can cease, and there can be peace in the valley.

Oh, So That's What That Means

And God called the light Day, and the darkness *He* called Night. And the evening and the morning were the first day.

—Genesis 1:5 (KJV)

This is the first time God's gender is disclosed. The fact that it refers to God as a *He* does not mean that the writer was a chauvinist, yet it establishes a working point from which we can start to establish some things about the Creator. Now, I know this is dangerous territory because you have the extremist who wants to take things too far and say, "Well, where did God come from? And how do we know God exists?" Well, I have two answers to that question. First of all, how do you know there was a George Washington? You know it because history records it. Moses, who wrote the first five books of the Bible, was responsible for giving us our origin. Everything that happened pre–Adam and Eve, well, I couldn't care less. It's like people saying Henry Ford invented the automobile, although he didn't, but the fact that it gives us a reference point of origin for someone who improved on it is good. I mainly want to know that when I crank up the vehicle that I drive now, it's safe and will get me to where I need to go. That's what's important to me. My second response is to those wannabe super-inquisitive doubters.

It reminds me of a little girl who went to school after summer break, and the teacher said for the first day back, that he wanted everyone to get up in front of the class and tell one thing they learned on summer vacation. This one little girl got up in front of the class and said, "I learned that there was a preacher named Jonah, whom God told to go to a city named Nineveh and preach, but Jonah didn't want to go, so he ran the opposite direction and got on a ship going to Tarshish, and the ship ran into a storm, and the captain and crew cast lots to see who would get thrown overboard. Jonah said, "I'm the cause of the storm. Throw me overboard." And they did, and he was swallowed up by a whale. After three days, he repented, and the whale vomited him up on dry land. He went to finish what God told him to do."

The teacher laughed and said, "That's a cute little story, young lady, but that couldn't dare be true. The throat of a whale is way too small to swallow a man."

She said, "Well, when I get to Heaven, I will ask Jonah."

The teacher replied, "But what if he went to Hell?"

She said, "Well, you ask him."

In Genesis 1:27, we discover language that could be misinterpreted if not understood clearly. In this passage, it says that He created man in His own image, and then we get into gender specificity, for the Bible says, "In the image of God created he him; male and female created he them." Does that means He created them at the same time, or was this some kind of bad prototype? No, not at all. Let's investigate.

> And the LORD God said, It is not good that the man should be alone; I will make him an help meet for him.
>
> Genesis 2:18 (KJV)

Wait a cotton-picking minute. I thought He made us in Genesis 1:27. And the answer is, yes, He did. So why is it mentioned again in Genesis 2:18? Well, you must understand that when people create something before they make it, they sit down and map it out before they actually bring it into manifestation. It's the thoughts of the Creator put into a blueprint, or what is commonly known now as the drawings. You never build something without a blueprint. The blueprint is the mind of the Creator sketched as to have a projected scale of dimensions. Drawings are a drafted look at the actual design. You see, my sister, you were on His mind in chapter 1 in the design stage as He put His thoughts on paper, symbolically speaking, then you went from God's mentality to becoming a reality. You were not an afterthought but a forethought. So, after chapter 1, He put His plans into action, and by the time we get to chapter 2, He made the necessary corrections, and then He brought you forth. Yet you are different by design. Notice that He said "male" and "female." Both are males—but not the same. You are *fe*male and a *wo*man. You see, you are the softer side of God. Whether we want to admit it or not, every man has an affinity for femininity. You girls are our softer side, a reflection of us with exceptions, and they are amazing and anatomical. You're equipped differently. Every positive needs a negative, every plus needs a minus, and every up needs a down. You are *fe*male, which means you are a male who can carry a fetus, and you are a *wo*man, a man who has a womb. Now that you are in shock mode that I called you a male and a man, let's put it in perspective—you were created with help and meet in mind. In other words, you were literally the answer to a prayer.

> [27] So God created man in his *own* image, in the image of God created he him; male and female created he them.
>
> [28] And God blessed them, and God said unto them, Be fruitful, and multiply, and replenish the earth, and subdue it: and have dominion over the fish of the sea, and over the fowl of the air, and over every living thing that moveth upon the earth.
>
> Genesis 1:27–28 (KJV)

It's *All* Good—Trust and Believe

³¹ And God saw everything that he had made, and, behold, *it was* very good. And the evening and the morning were the sixth day.

—Genesis 1:31 (KJV)

I love language, as you'll learn later in this section. Words tell you what they want you know. The Master Craftsman shifts or changes gears on us, if you will. He went from creating to using the word "made."

He started off creating, then He went to speaking and saying, "Let there be," then He went to bringing forth, and all of these terms refer to the creation of the planet and the cosmos. Yet when it came to you and me, He said, "Let us make." Up until this point, He spoke to things and spoke out things. That's important because whenever God created something, He spoke to what He was making it out of. When He got ready to make the grass, He spoke to the ground. When He got ready to make fish, He spoke to the water. When He got ready to make man, He spoke to himself. And whatever He created, it must stay connected to what He made it out of if it wants to live. For instance, if grass wants to live, it has to stay connected to the ground; if fish want to live, they have to stay connected to the water; and if mankind wants to live, he and she must stay connected to God. So he made us with us staying connected in mind.

When you make something, you have to put your hands on it and get involved with it. When I was a little boy and momma said she was going to make a cake, she would first gather the ingredients. This within itself was a process that required thought and skill because she needed to know how much or how little of each to make it turn out and taste right. Then she needed the skill to know when to put in what and how much time you had to leave it in the oven. And if you are old school like me, you normally had to go outside, because if you didn't, for some reason the cake would fall if too much jumping and running went on. But she had to use her hands to make the cake—not *bake* the cake; that took heat to bake it. But it took her hands to *make* it. The fact that he said, "Let us make man," and it says, "Made he them male and female." Well, that simply means that he put his hands on us.

There Is Too Much to Celebrate, Not Criticize

We are so important to Him that He didn't entrust the task to anyone but Himself. We were on His mind because He made us in His image, which is a reflection of oneself. That's why they call us a masterpiece, because we are all pieces of the Master. However, before we go forward, I need you to know that God wasn't a woman, but He wasn't a chauvinist either. You see, because He's a master builder, He thought out every single detail of humankind. Do you remember when I said earlier that words matter and that I love language? Well, this is why.

When it comes to your womanhood, you are different by design, which makes you not our other half but the best half. This is the first time in scripture God gives a benediction—not in the sense of the final words by the pastor at the end of a church service. Come here, girlfriend. "Bene" means "good" and "diction" means "words"—good words. When He says in Genesis 1:31 that everything He made was good and very good, that was a benediction. In Genesis 2:18 we see the first malediction ("mal" means "not good," and "diction" again means "words").

> 18 And the LORD God said, *It is* not good that the man should be alone; I will make him an help meet for him.

Genesis 2:18 (KJV)

This is the first time He gives a malediction over His creation because the final stroke needed to complete the canvas of mankind was missing. You weren't there, and it was not a good look. You matter so much, that your absence made the Master change His language. As a result, He saved the best for last. He put Adam, which means first to sleep, and brought forth Eve.

> 21 And the LORD God caused a deep sleep to fall upon Adam, and he slept: and he took one of his ribs, and closed up the flesh instead thereof;
>
> 22 And the rib, which the LORD God had taken from man, made he a woman, and brought her unto the man.
>
> 23 And Adam said, This *is* now bone of my bones, and flesh of my flesh: she shall be called Woman, because she was taken out of Man.
>
> 24 Therefore shall a man leave his father and his mother, and shall cleave unto his wife: and they shall be one flesh.
>
> 25 And they were both naked, the man and his wife, and were not ashamed.

Genesis 2:21–25 (KJV)

Eve means "life giver." In this passage, we see the first medical procedure. God, the divine anesthesiologist, puts man under, and with precision, He brings forth a rib, and brought forth a woman out of the man, and subsequently, every man from that point on came out of a woman. We also saw the first wedding vows and marriage ceremony as God instituted marriage. Look at how much your creation—women brought about. It's all good because you're here.

CHAPTER 2

Got Milk?
The FDA Lied—We Need 'Em

In this culture, very rarely do we investigate what things mean. Outside of Google or asking Jeeves about something, 98 percent of the population accepts things as they always were without question or interrogatory thought. For instance, have you ever wondered why or where we get the terms "momma," "mom," and "mother"? Well, you women carry the answer. The breast derives from the word "mammary" from the Latin word "mamma." It's all centered on your breast. You see, men have breasts also, but we lack the ability to lactate.

Mamma (plural *mammas) Alternative spelling of* mama: mother.

From Latin mamma (*plural* mammae *or* mammas)

(*Anatomy*) The milk-secreting organ of female humans and other mammals which includes the mammary gland and the nipple or teat; a breast; an udder. (*plural:* mammae)

(*Meteorology*) **an accessory cloud like a mammary in appearance, which can form on the underside of most cloud general** 1. *Wikipedia,* last modified July 18, 2008, http://en.wikipedia.org/wiki/Style_guide.

What I want most for women around the world to carry away from this offering of mine to the literary world is that you matter so much. God made you with a plan in mind. We need you, and we can't make it without you. So before I get into the good stuff, allow me to set the table.

Do you remember when they used to have all these commercials with famous stars from the film industry to the sports world with a milk mustache, saying, "Got milk?" Well, it was a marketing gold mine. The milk industry sold us—yes, we, the great American society a superpower and mega-intelligent society in the known world—a big fat *lie!*

Yes, they told us that we need more calcium and that we needed to drink more milk with vitamin D, and then the ads came. Everyone from superstars to supermodels and from professional athletes to the financial elite was sporting a milk mustache. So what did we do? We responded, of course. We went out and loaded up on milk. Now, some years later, all of a sudden, half the population we've discovered is lactose intolerant.

So, here is the truth—yes, it was the truth clothed in a lie. The merchant world knows that those of us who live in this entertainment-hungry society don't think, or as we say, "Don't ask, don't tell" and so we don't have that old interrogative and inquisitive desire to ask why anymore.

I've always been inquisitive because my parents taught my siblings and me to be thinkers. Aretha Franklin said it best in the lyrics of a song, "You better think—think about what they are trying to do to you. You better think, think about freedom" ….. well, you get the picture—for those who know the song.

You know the rest. Well, here's how they got us, and then I'll tell you what they got us on.

There is a word called 'muse. It means "to think."

Then, if you put the prefix 'a,' which means "not to" in front of it, you get "amuse"—not to think. That is what amusement parks are designed to do—basically, to get you not to think. Have you ever noticed that when you go to an amusement park, time flies by, and you spend a whole day and a whole lot of money because you have been amused by the rides and roller coasters and games and food and fun, so much so until you were oblivious to the fact that it arrested you from the reality that you are being distracted from thinking? Don't get me wrong, I am not antifun: We need to turn off the old thinker and just get lost in the moment every now and then. Yet, when that's over, you'd better put back on your thinking cap and not stay in euphoria.

It's been said that what you don't know won't hurt you, but I believe the stuff that you don't think about can kill you. Most milk in the supermarket is from cows. The Food and Drug Administration (FDA) told us that we needed more calcium (please tell me why food and drugs are not separate. It's probably because most of our foods are laced and loaded with synthetic drugs. So the food and drug industries are in bed together, and that is why the powers that be regulate food in a nonagrarian society). Years ago, in the '40s and '50s, that would have been fine, but as the population grew, the need to feed the population grew also. To make a long story short, you put all your farmers out of business, develop chemicals to speed up everything to keep up with demand, and so now we have sixty-two chemicals in a honey bun. Most of us can't pronounce the names of the ingredients, yet we put this poison in our bodies and wonder why one in three Americans has cancer. Or you rush chickens, which normally take six months to grow to frying size with a grain-fed diet, to now six weeks on a chemical food diet. Think, people—if the chemical gets in the chicken, it also gets in the egg. When we eat either, the chemicals also get into us. When I was growing up, they used to say, "You are what you eat." That's another story. Couple that with the dyes in all the sugary fruit drinks and sodas that we ingest and now our kids are diagnosed with ADD and ADHD. Are you serious? No one heard of these diseases thirty years ago. Then, on top of that, we send our kids to school, not with a hot breakfast, but with a bowl of cereal so loaded with sugar and glucose that it's like pouring milk over a bowl of candy. By the time they get to school, the teacher can't gain control because the kids are bouncing off the walls from the sugar rush.

Sorry I got on that one. Back to the milk.

So they told us a truth dressed up in lies. Let me show you how it works. You see, a five-minute lie is easier to believe than a five-hour lie. So let's just say it's 6:15 p.m. on a Tuesday before dinner, and you ask me what time it is, and I say, "Oh, it's 6:20 p.m." Well, you wouldn't think much about it because it's a five-minute lie. However, if I say, "It's 11:15 p.m.," you would think I had lost my mind because you will believe a five-minute lie before you believe a five-hour lie.

So, television and Hollywood keep us amused with what I call not-my-reality TV, which is nothing but a bunch of five-minute lies. Then they sprinkle in three minutes of commercials—which, by the way, are lies, as well. So we are saturated with all these lies that look true. So, if our stars whom we idolize say it's true, then it must be true, right? *Wrong.*

So That's How They Got Us to Believe It. This Is What They Got Us to Believe.

The presently poison-riddled American diet has led us to become a society that now faces a child obesity crisis and a type 2 diabetes norm. It's mainly the fact that we consume calories we don't need because we are gluttonous. I confess that I am guilty too. Then our kids no longer go outside and play because it's not safe, and they have an iPad and video games galore, which includes everything from DSs, Wiis, and Game Boys, and oh, five-year-olds now need iPhones. You don't have a job, can't really read yet, but you have a data plan? Someone explain to me what is really going on.

The FDA said we need milk, and so it must be true because everybody from Michael Jordan to Michael Jackson and Taylor Swift to Tyra Banks has a milk mustache on commercials, billboards, newspapers, and magazines across the country saying, "Got Milk?" Ads went up all over the world—billions of dollars were spent, and hundreds of billions were made on that campaign. And, yes, we need milk for strong bones, right? *Wrong*.

Here's the *Truth*

We need our mother's milk for strong bones and calcium. You see, baby cows needs their mothers' milk because they have to gain 150 pounds in their first year of life in order to survive. So, to be healthy, a baby calf needs its mother's milk. But, if you give cow's milk to humans, what do you think happens?

We blow up too. So why would you give us cow's milk for calcium and then pasteurize it and cook all the nutrients out so it won't spoil?

Here's the truth they didn't tell you. There is more calcium in a plate or serving of collard greens than there is in a whole gallon of milk.

We no longer subscribe to being how God created us to be. The dinner table is extinct; we no longer sit around it. The place that used to be for the family to commune and consume a meal has diminished. Dinner is now served out of a bag through a window prepared by the hands of strangers. Mothers, we need you and your breasts. We need your milk for our babies. It may be inconvenient, and it may be frustrating if the baby will not latch on right away. It may take a while for the baby to get the hang of it because the child just got here and this is all new, but your baby will be healthier and less at risk of disease if you give him or her breast milk. You must also eat healthy while you're pregnant. By breast-feeding, you'll also save money and get more sleep.

According to the World Health Organization (WHO), breast-feeding is one of the most effective ways to ensure child health and survival. If every child was breast-fed within an hour of birth and was given only breast milk for their first six months of life and continued breast-feeding up to the age of two years old, about 220,000 lives would be saved every year. Globally, fewer than 40 percent of infants under the age of six months are exclusively breast-fed. Breast-feeding counseling and support are essential for increasing this percentage. Here are some facts you may want to consider if you are a soon to be mother, or planning a pregnancy, or know someone who could use this information:

Health Benefits for Infants

Breast milk is the ideal food for newborns and infants. It gives infants all the nutrients they need for healthy development. It is safe and contains antibodies that help protect infants from common childhood illnesses such as diarrhea and pneumonia—the two primary causes of child mortality worldwide. Breast milk is readily available and affordable, which helps to ensure that infants get adequate nutrition.

Benefits for Mothers

Breastfeeding also benefits mothers. Exclusive breastfeeding is associated with a natural (though not fail-safe) method of birth control (98 percent protection in the first six months after birth). It reduces risks of breast and ovarian cancer later in life, helps women return to their pre-pregnancy weight faster, and lowers rates of obesity.

Long-term Benefits for Children

Beyond the immediate benefits for children, breastfeeding contributes to a lifetime of good health. Adolescents and adults who were breastfed as babies are less likely to be overweight or obese. They are less likely to have type 2 diabetes and perform better in intelligence tests.

Why Not Infant Formula?

Infant formula does not contain the antibodies found in breast milk. When infant formula is not properly prepared, there are risks arising from the use of unsafe water and unsterilized equipment or the potential presence of bacteria in powdered formula. Malnutrition can result from over-diluting formula to "stretch" supplies. While frequent feeding maintains breast milk supply, if formula is used but becomes unavailable, a return to breastfeeding may not be an option due to diminished breast milk production.

Support for Mothers is Essential

Breastfeeding is a learned skill set and many women encounter difficulties at the beginning. Pain in the nipple and fear that there is not enough milk to sustain the baby are common. Health facilities that support breastfeeding—

by making trained breastfeeding counselors available to new mothers—encourage higher rates of the practice. To provide this support and improve care for mothers and newborns, there are "baby-friendly" facilities in about 152 countries thanks to the WHO-UNICEF Baby-friendly Hospital Initiative.

I'm just asking you to think—the world needs breasts and what they deliver. God knew what He was doing when he created woman as He did.

I know that sometimes telling people the truth can be hazardous because we have developed a society that has enabled us to become superficial and artificial and we no longer desire the real thing. We substitute the truth every day, and yet teach our kids not to lie to us, but we feed them lies and perpetrate lies about ourselves daily—everything from fake hair and weaves to acrylic nails and colored contact lenses. It's as if the lie of having artificial things on us has gotten in us.

My daddy used to say that a lie is halfway around the world before truth gets up and put its shoes on.

I'm just asking you to *think*. We need 'em—breasts—and we need what's in them. God knew what he was doing.

CHAPTER 3

Onions Don't Cry
Everything Has Purpose

It's interesting to me how we don't love ourselves like we should. There's more self-hate and self-rejection going on in this world than any other type of abuse. The Bible says, "Love thy neighbor as you love yourself." But how can you love your neighbor as yourself when you don't love yourself?

My sisters you are so amazing. I wish I could tell you that the creator made you from the rib, but that's not true. He made you from the prime rib. You are the lifeline of humanity. Without you—yes, *you*—we cease to be a society, and if you stop being what God created you to be, in approximately 120 years from this very day that you are reading this book, *we would all die off* and be no more. That is how powerful you are.

A story is told of a young lady who went off to college. When she had been there awhile, she was discouraged that her grades weren't where they should be, and she wanted to quit. On top of that, she had a horrible social life and was so overwhelmed that she wrote to her mother, who was poor and didn't have much, and said, "Momma, I'm ready to commit suicide. This world doesn't need me. I have no friends, my grades are low, and I stay depressed so much so that I can't even cry anymore because I have no more tears."

Her mother was so hurt when she received the letter that she got on a train and mustered up enough money to pay her daughter a visit. When she arrived at her daughter's dorm, she knocked on the door, and her daughter opened the door to her utter surprise. She said, "Momma, what are you doing here?"

Her mother walked past her without saying a word and went to her little kitchenette and said, "Sit down, girl." Her mother proceeded to pull an onion out of a little greasy bag. She said, "Baby, whenever you feel insignificant, I want you to think of this onion. Nobody says very much about the onion, unlike the apple. People loved the apple so much that they wrote a jingle and said, "An apple a day keeps the doctor away" but not the onion. When we catch colds, people rush to the store and buy oranges because of their vitamin C, but not the onion. However, the onion doesn't complain that it's not as popular or lauded as the apple or orange is. The onion just holds its own because it knows that you can't make a proper stew, chili, or soup unless you get you an onion. You can't even have a hamburger that's flavorful unless you season it with onion. Some recipes are incomplete unless you add onion, and although you can make all of those things without an onion, it still won't taste the same. Yet the onion holds a gift that no other fruit or vegetable can boost."

The daughter asked, "What's that, momma?"

Her mother said, "I've never seen an onion cry, but I've seen it make many people cry."

So, baby, be encouraged—onions don't cry.

That's how valuable you are. I speak even unto my lesbian sisters. I wish I could love you back into embracing your true femininity, whether you were violated or molested or raped or abused. I've seen too many times the ills of a sick, plagued male society that passed more laws to protect the criminal than the victim. So many of you may feel uncovered, so I hear you loud and clear when you say that you would rather buy a sex toy or apparatus and lie in the arms of another woman who understands you and who you feel won't harm you because she understands. The truth of the matter is that I'm not your judge, so I won't condemn you, although I may not condone it. But, you were purposefully made.

You were not made to be a second-class citizen or the property of a man for his pleasure and then discarded after he's had his fun and done his business on top of you. I just want you to know you don't have to shave off your hair and tape down your breasts, sag your pants or take hormones and have a deep voice or even get a sex change to look like a male or feel like a man.

Just know that you were made in that body with breasts for a reason. Girlfriend, you are the nurturer of society. Whatever you give a woman, she gives it back to you multiplied. If we give you a seed, you give us a baby. If we give you groceries, you give us a meal. If we give you a house, you turn it into a home. Whatever you touch is better after being exposed to you. You give Madam C. J. Walker some home remedies and a scalp disease, and she'll give you a sulfur shampoo and the first self-made female millionaire. You give an Albanian nurse named Teresa sick and poor people for forty-five years, and she'll give you healed orphans and a Nobel Peace Prize. You give a virgin named Mary a night with the Holy Ghost, and she will give the savior of the whole round world the only begotten son of

God. You give a tired schoolteacher and seamstress a seat on a bus in a segregated society, and she will give you a civil rights movement that birthed the likes of a Martin Luther King Jr. Give a little black girl from Mississippi a communications degree and a news anchor job, and she will give you the *Oprah Winfrey Show* and the OWN Network. All I'm saying is whatever you touch changes, and we're waiting on your story because onions don't cry. You also have something as a woman that no one else can do like you. I apologize that there have been some sick male individuals who have soiled the fabric of humanity and turned some of our sisters out to resent the packages they arrived in. But that earth suit of yours sets you aside. You were built to be the progenitors and nurturers of all the races of the earth. So celebrate your womanhood. Breasts mean life.

And remember, onions don't cry, but they make people cry!

Knowing your CUP size is not about size; it's about significance.

CHAPTER 4

The C stands for _ _ _ _ _ _ _

And we know that all things work together for good to them that love God, to them who are the called according to his purpose.

—Romans 8:28 (KJV)

from the same as (klesis); ***invited***, i.e. ***appointed***, or (special) a ***saint*** :- called.

The C stands for "calling." Every woman needs to know her calling. Yes, you, my sister, were called, from the original Greek word meaning "invited." You didn't just show up as a freeloader, moocher, or leech. You were sent for, summoned, invited, and appointed, which means there's a place for you. With specificity, God called you for His divine intervention in human affairs.

Now, please understand that a calling requires two things: first, there is the *responsibility* on and of the one who does the calling. Then there is the *response* from the one being called. For instance, we just learned the origin of the word "called" comes from the word "invited." Let's just say I invite you over to my home for dinner. Well, I have now a responsibility to make sure I provide a nice, clean environment and ambiance in which to eat. Then, there is the responsibility for me to provide the meal and all the trimmings, such as beverage and dessert; knives, forks—well, you get the picture. As the inviter, that becomes my responsibility. As the recipient to my request, you then have the ability to decline or respond by your presence and bringing your appetite.

However, when God called you, He called or invited us to be a part of His purpose. As a woman who needs to know her CUP size, you need to get this in your spirit if nothing else. You were called to be a part of God's ultimate purpose. You were called to something greater than yourself and not just your own personal agenda. So, I'm sorry to disappoint you, but your life is more than pedis and manis and finding the man of your dreams and having your little picket fence in the suburbs; and life is more than just the latest Louis Vuitton and Michael Kors bag; or the latest, greatest fad, trend, or style. Those things are accoutrements while here on earth, but none of them are necessities. You were called to be a part of the Creator's agenda, His divine plan. Thus, he has a responsibility, and you bare the burden to respond to the invitation.

Stick to the Script

The problem I have with overly religious and spiritual people is that they over spiritualize things. Now, don't get me wrong, I'm very clear. God is Spirit, and they that worship him, you must worship him in spirit and in truth. However, God chooses to work through human agents. So you can say, "Well, I don't follow man, I'm following God," but you don't know what God is doing unless He's doing it through someone. You've been called according to God's plan. Therefore, all things work together for the good. Now I don't have time for a theology lesson, but the words "work together" are a whole term in Greek—"synergos," where we get our word "synergy." Synergy is defined as simply two forces working together without regard to their relationship on a spectrum. My own definition of synergy is where two things from opposite sides of the spectrum come together to work on a common project. God is a divine scientist who takes your good and your bad, your ups, and your downs, your tragedies and your triumphs; pain and joy, hope and despair and makes them work together on your own personal project called "project for my good."

Yes, I know that some people want all flowers and no trees, all honey and no bees, but the truth of the matter is that when you know you have been invited, the one who did the inviting has something planned for your arrival.

You've got to understand that your calling is so sealed to work for your good that you will miss it if you stop reading there. Let me give you a little secret about the Bible. The Bible used to be a scroll, meaning that we didn't get verses and chapters until, like, the 1500s. So, you must remember that verses and chapters are there for reference's sake and benchmarks, not necessarily to separate. So watch what he says as the Apostle Paul closes out the chapter.

> [29] For whom he did foreknow, he also did predestinate *to be* conformed to the image of his Son, that he might be the firstborn among many brethren.
>
> [30] Moreover whom he did predestinate, them he also called: and whom he called, them he also justified: and whom he justified, them he also glorified.
>
> [31] What shall we then say to these things? If God *be* for us, who *can be* against us?

32 He that spared not his own Son, but delivered him up for us all, how shall he not with him also freely give us all things?

33 Who shall lay any thing to the charge of God's elect? *It is* God that justifieth.

34 Who *is* he that condemneth? *It is* Christ that died, yea rather, that is risen again, who is even at the right hand of God, who also maketh intercession for us.

35 Who shall separate us from the love of Christ? *shall* tribulation, or distress, or persecution, or famine, or nakedness, or peril, or sword?

36 As it is written, For thy sake we are killed all the day long; we are accounted as sheep for the slaughter.

37 Nay, in all these things we are more than conquerors through him that loved us.

38 For I am persuaded, that neither death, nor life, nor angels, nor principalities, nor powers, nor things present, nor things to come,

39 Nor height, nor depth, nor any other creature, shall be able to separate us from the love of God, which is in Christ Jesus our Lord.

Romans 8:29–39 (KJV)

Notice the language. He said, "Those whom he did foreknow," which means whom He knew before, "he did predestinate." Bishop Jakes breaks this down phenomenally by saying that "pre" means "before" and "destinate" means "end," so He knew our ending before our beginning. It's what Hollywood does in movies—they shoot the final scenes first and then go back and shoot the beginning and the middle because they know how it's going to turn out. So, although you and I are sitting there biting our nails in suspense, the producers are relaxing because they knew how it was going to turn out before they started. So it is with the One Who invited us here to earth. God doesn't panic because He knows how your movie is going to turn out. There will be nail-biting moments, but relax. The One Who wrote your story has a plot that will blow your mind.

I remember having surgery once. I never was big on doctors and hospitals. Not long after I was released from recovery, they sent me to my room and soon afterward, they sent an LPN into my room to take me for a walk. The young lady (whose name slips me at the moment) said in a bold, demanding voice, "Mr. Bond, I'm here to take you for a walk."

I said, "This must be a mistake. I just came out of surgery."

She said, "No, sir, the doctors want you up walking as soon as possible."

Well, that wasn't my problem. It was the fact that she was, at best, 95 pounds soaking wet, and I was 553 pounds at the time so I told her, "Well, who's going to help you?"

She said, "No one. Now, I'm going to help you out of bed, and I want you to trust and put all your weight on me."

I then thought not only was this a joke, but that she must also have been blind or she was about to make the worst decision of her life.

So I asked, "Why would you want me to first, trust you to walk a man my size, but then, you ask me to put all my weight on you?"

And what she said earned my respect for the duration of my stay and the rest of our walks—she exclaimed, "First, I've been doing this a long time, and second, I've never dropped one yet!"

Girlfriend, knowing your CUP size requires a faith that says, "God, I trust that sense you called me. I'm gonna put my weight on you, because you've been God a long time, and last I checked, you've never dropped one yet."

There is no "happily ever after" without first a "once upon a time," but if you get caught up in "once upon a time" and get stuck there, you will never realize that if you keep living, "happily ever after" is on the way. According to Psalm 30:5 weeping endures but a night, but joy cometh in the morning. Even when it's still dark at 11:59 p.m., people are still saying good night, but at 12:00 a.m., it's still dark, and folks start saying good morning. Let's look at it in the Eugene Peterson version:

> 29 God knew what he was doing from the very beginning. He decided from the outset to shape the lives of those who love him along the same lines as the life of his Son. The Son stands first in the line of humanity he restored. We see the original and intended shape of our lives there in him.

> 30 After God made that decision of what his children should be like, he followed it up by calling people by name. After he called them by name, he set them on a solid

basis with himself. And then, after getting them established, he stayed with them to the end, gloriously completing what he had begun.

31 So, what do you think? With God on our side like this, how can we lose?

32 If God didn't hesitate to put everything on the line for us, embracing our condition and exposing himself to the worst by sending his own Son, is there anything else he wouldn't gladly and freely do for us?

33 And who would dare tangle with God by messing with one of God's chosen?

34 Who would dare even to point a finger? The One who died for us—who was raised to life for us!—is in the presence of God at this very moment sticking up for us.

35 Do you think anyone is going to be able to drive a wedge between us and Christ's love for us? There is no way! Not trouble, not hard times, not hatred, not hunger, not homelessness, not bullying threats, not backstabbing, not even the worst sins listed in Scripture:

36 They kill us in cold blood because they hate you. We're sitting ducks; they pick us off one by one.

37 None of this fazes us because Jesus loves us.

38 I'm absolutely convinced that nothing—nothing living or dead, angelic or demonic, today or tomorrow,

39 high or low, thinkable or unthinkable—absolutely *nothing* can get between us and God's love because of the way that Jesus our Master has embraced us.

Romans 8:29–39 (MSG)

Stick With the Script!

You've got to know your calling. What you've been called to, and, as I will discuss shortly, to whom you've been called. Life is like an elevator full of ups and downs, but pain is the birthmark of a believer. One of my preaching contemporaries, Pastor Bertrand Bailey, talks about in a sermon that best sums up what I'm saying. He tells about how, when he was a boy, he used to love to watch *Batman*. Before this modern-day Batman, there was a day when Batman had a sidekick named Robin, and they would get into some tight, tumultuous predicaments and situations and sometimes fall into the hands of the sinister crime syndicate headed by the Joker and all his minions. But, no matter what would happen, and no matter how bad things looked, Batman and Robin would always, in the nick of time, come out on top. One day, the young Bertrand Bailey asked his daddy after a near-heart-clinching episode, how they made it out every time. His father said, "Son, you can't see it, but behind the camera, there is a guy holding up these cards called cue cards with the script written on them. And as long as they stick with the script, they will win in the end every time."

Oh, I get excited about the fact that, if we just stick with the script that the writer, the author, and finisher of our faith has written, we will come out a winner every time because we've been called, and it's at His invitation that we must respond, and if we do, who can be against us?

Once you know that you have been called, you need to know to whom you have been called. I will deal with some of that later, but also remember that *C* stands for something else, as well.

The C Also Stands for Cost

Girlfriend, you've got to also know your cost—not price, because you're not for sale. It is when you have counted up your value and when you understand your own self-worth that you wake up and not allow your value to be determined by others. Now, please understand that "calling" and "cost" are synonymous. When you understand the cost of woman-hood, you value your sisterhood differently because you value yourself differently. You begin to understand that free doesn't mean cheap. You see if you invite me over for dinner and I offer to bring something and you say, "No, just bring your appetite," well, I get to enjoy a free meal. But even though it's free to me, it cost you something. You had to buy the groceries and pay for the utensils and utilities. Oh, yes, it cost somebody. That is why you must understand the cost. You pay a price to be who you are, where you are, and what you are. That's why you should never allow anyone to cheapen your presence and devalue your body or your brains. You are more than lips, hips, and fingertips. You may be a brick house, but you also come with furniture. You are not an empty piece of real estate waiting for someone to come along and occupy. It cost you something, and don't be shy about letting those who wish to enjoy your time, company, gifting, and presence know that there is a cost involved.

Yes, I admire women of all shapes and sizes, colors, ethnicities, backgrounds, and so on. Yet, I understand that the cost to be a woman is a price that we men can't afford. I am neither equipped nor do I desire to trade places with a woman in situations like childbirth and labor pains—the adjustment and transformation of the body costs more than I think I could pay. You see, sister, your most valuable asset is not what's between your legs, but what's between your ears. You are not a whore, harlot, or female dog, but you are the epitome of virtuousness.

And I don't care about your past—not in the sense that I am saying it's not relevant because it is—but remember that you are called, and your cost is valued far above rubies. You are not your mistake, you are not your past, and you are not your last sexual encounter. You are not your sex partner's pleasure toy—you are a valuable vessel who adds value to all whom you encounter.

I remember hearing the story of a first black mayor of Chicago—one of our large US cities. On his way home one night, he and his wife, the first lady of the city, pulled into a full-service filling station. You remember those if you were a '70s baby. Full-service gas stations were where an attendant would come out, and you could sit in the comfort of your car while being serviced. My, how things were much slower and better back in those days. But anyway, while you were sitting there, an attendant would come and ask you how much gas you wanted, and he would proceed to pump your fuel, check your oil level, cap off any fluids if need be, and also clean your windshield. Well, this particular evening, the mayor and his wife sat at the pump, and when the attendant pumped the gas, he came around the front of the car and began to clean the windshield. And when the mayor's wife saw him, she was startled as if she had seen a ghost, and jumped lightly.

Her inquisitive husband asked, "What's wrong, honey?"

She reluctantly said, "Well, that gentleman who's cleaning our windshield was my first love."

He then snickered and said, "Wow, I guess you're glad you didn't marry him."

She asked, "Why do you say that?"

He said, "Because you wouldn't be married to the first black mayor of Chicago, and you wouldn't be the First Lady of this great city."

She said, "Oh, yes, I would have."

He asked, "Well, how's that?"

She said, "If I had married him, *he* would have been the first black mayor of Chicago."

Her point was that she understood her calling, and she knew that she was the one pushing him on when he wanted to quit, reassuring him and cheerleading from the stands. So she was an asset, never a liability.

To Whom Are You Called?

What a complexity of sorts. The million-dollar question—you had to have seen it coming—the question we all have been waiting on. "Charles Bond, how do I get the man of my dreams?" Well, slow down, my sister, this particular section is not necessarily about you being Barbie and me telling you how to get Ken. I also won't waste your time by being or playing matchmaker like I'm some sort of clergy cupid. However, I would like to bring some clarity to this very broad spectrum because there is so much advice out there. Allow me to say that I dare not be a small fish in the large pond of relationship advice. However, let's not fool ourselves. I've been told that most little girls start planning their weddings as young as twelve years of age, so it's safe to say that most women desire a mate (as do men, as well) And, yes, this is so natural because, remember, it's not good for us to be alone. That's not to suggest that singleness is a curse. Yet, we were created to cross-pollinate and coagulate in pairs. But I warn you, it's of utmost importance to know to whom you are called, as well. So my question is, are you ready?

Let's Have a Funeral at the Wedding`

In the spring of 2012, the nation's news was interrupted by the reports that an unarmed seventeen-year-old kid was shot and killed by an adult who allegedly mistook him for a criminal. I dare not take this time to express personal feelings for the tension of the moment and the events that followed what is now known as the Trayvon Martin case. However, this event showed the true fabric of race relations and moral rectitude—or shall I say lack thereof, in a nation that is supposed to be leader among nations. Needless to say, I will just leave it alone by concluding that we, as a nation, have a long way to go when we send the message that it's alright to kill unarmed kids on assumptions. Also, no matter what the race of the pursuant or the pursued, we must realize that the blood that flows within us and that was shed for us, should always be thicker than the race and space that divides us.

After this incident, I took some of the kids from my church to lunch to have a roundtable discussion to see where their little heads were. I wanted to know the effects it had on our kids. So, as we sat around the table, I heard all kinds of emotions from fear to anger. Following the meal, I asked my admin to accompany us to the movies to help supervise the small group. When we arrived at the theater in the Easton Mall here in Columbus, Ohio, I purchased our tickets and we moved toward the escalator that would eventually lead to our theater. I led the small group up to the ticket taker, who was a handicapped gentleman and was well stricken in years. He also had some kind of physical disability and I really admired the fact that, at his age, he did not let his physical limitations hinder him from living. As we approached, because he saw me, three kids, and my admin, he assumed we were a family, and said with his slurred speech, "How did you get so lucky to find someone that pretty to put up with you?"

We all chuckled, but my admin, Alisha, responded, "Oh no, that's not my husband, that's my pastor."

He then proceeded to apologize and we reassured him that no offense was taken. And me and my wanting-to-be-quick-witted self, noticed a wedding band on his ring finger; I asked him in turn who or how did he find someone to put up with him, in a humorous manner.

He resounded proudly, "Fifty-four years I've been married to the same woman." We all had a look of mud on our faces, because in a society where some folks can't stay together fifty-four *days*, we were all just in awe. He proclaimed his undying love for his bride of over a half a century as though he were a newlywed.

"Well, how *did* you find someone to put up with you that long?" I asked him before we went up to see our movie, returning his own form of humor as I chuckled, subliminally saying that two could play that game. The words I heard will change my life forever. I never got his name, but what came out of his mouth next changed my view on mates and marriage for the rest of my human life. He said this:

"Well, I will tell you the secret. We didn't have a wedding, we had a funeral. I died to myself, and she died to herself, and we both died to Christ."

I was speechless. All the sermons I had preached, all the counseling I had attempted, and all of the advice I had given over twenty-plus years as a minister—I felt like a hypocrite who needed to find every couple I had ever performed a ceremony for and repent and beg their forgiveness for not telling them the most important part was not something borrowed or something blue; and that it was not something old or something new, but I wanted to repent for not telling them that the key to making it work was not having a wedding but having a funeral.

Yes, you will find that to whom you are called will eventually become less about whether they are tall, dark, and handsome or short, fat, and ugly. It is not always about whether they had wealth or riches and certainly not about their abilities to prove their sexual prowess. Yet it all boils down to not whether you can change them or they can change you but, rather, if you are both willing to have a funeral on your wedding day.

Practicality, Prayer, Preparation: The Three *P*s

I have a confession (I feel like a gossip columnist): I really desire to be married. I must confess that I feel so out of sorts when I travel all over the country and attend functions and all of the other couples show up arm in arm. If I don't have a date, I feel so out of sorts and awkward. Now, don't get me wrong, I am a very eligible bachelor. Also, let me state that it's not that I don't have options or that some of my exes didn't make the cut. Truth be told, some of the women I've dated and courted were beautiful, gorgeous women who were and still are women I respect and admire. Most of all, whether they knew it then or not, I didn't feel adequate to be their husband, so the blame is more on me than them, and I'll own it: It was not that they weren't marriage material; however, I realize more and more that I have allowed fears and past relationships to weigh heavy on my decisions. Not that I haven't moved on, and not that I am allowing my past to dictate my future. I'm clear on that. Maybe I chose career over cohabitation, I don't know, but whatever the case, I have learned more about myself in the last year or so than I care to know. BOne of the principles that I teach is that prayer is good, practicality is great, but preparation is a must. I often say that God does not always give you what you pray for, but He gives you what you are prepared for. Sometimes, however, He will give us what we pray for to show us that we are not always ready for the things we are requesting.

The world-renowned pop star Beyoncé put out a song several years ago entitled, "Single Ladies (Put a Ring on It)." This song instantly shot up the charts and was listed at the top of the charts as number one for a record-breaking number of weeks. It quickly became the anthem of seemingly every single woman on the planet. However, I questioned the fact that every woman who desires a ring doesn't necessarily deserve a ring. In all actuality, ladies, let's be honest we must own the fact that getting the ring should never be more important than getting, keeping, and maintaining the man who presents the ring. If the delusion of getting the ring was so tantamount, then truth be told, you most likely could afford your own diamond ring. So, what the ring represents is more important, neither rock size nor carats determine reality or character.

So if you are going to know your CUP size, or shall I say, your calling, allow me to say something about these 3 *P* words.

Pray Like It's All Up to God, and Live Like It's All Up to You!

So let's start with prayer. Christianity, along with other religions from Buddhism to *Shaktism* emphatically teaches the importance of prayer. As a matter of fact, the Bible says man ought to always pray. And then in another place, it says to pray without ceasing. If you are in a true Bible-teaching church, then you also understand that prayer is not just an opportunity to get before God and treat him like a spiritual sugar daddy or a cosmic Santa Claus. Prayer is about not only meditation, but conversation with the Creator. He will give you revelation if you would only spend enough time in the conversation. Most of our prayers are about what we expect or desire from God and almost never what He expects from us, yet prayer is essential.

Yes, conversation with the Creator. I like to refer to it as touching base with the boss. It's like getting clearance from the tower before takeoff and then also getting clearance before touchdown, but also all throughout the day, because between take off and touchdown, you are going to experience some turbulence so you need prayer. In Matthew 6 nestled in the sermon on the mount—or more properly, shall I say the lesson on the mount— Jesus himself gives a prescription of sorts—a recipe, if you will—of what prayer ought to consist of.

> 5 And when thou prayest, thou shall not be as the hypocrites *are*: for they love to pray standing in the synagogues and in the corners of the streets, that they may be seen of men. Verily I say unto you, they have their reward.

> 6 But thou, when thou prayest, enter into thy closet, and when thou hast shut thy door, pray to thy Father which is in secret; and thy Father which seeth in secret shall reward thee openly.

7 But when ye pray, use not vain repetitions, as the heathen *do*: for they think that they shall be heard for their much speaking.

8 Be not ye therefore like unto them: for your Father knoweth what things ye have need of, before ye ask him.

Matthew 6:5–8 (KJV)

Look at how Jesus starts off by telling them what not to do. He says, in essence, "Let me help you avoid some of the asinine antics of those hypocrites." It's interesting that we say in our culture that a hypocrite is a person who says one thing and does another. That's not a hypocrite, that's a liar. A hypocrite comes from the words "hupo crites." "Hupo" means "under," and "crites" means "mask." Put it together, and it means from "under the mask." It is derived from the fact that in those days, they had theater, but not like we do today. They would make masks for whatever characters were in the play, and the actors and actresses would speak their parts from under the masks because they were acting like someone. Thus, the Master says, "Don't be like the hypocrites," or those who speak from under masks, because a hypocrite is not someone who says one thing and does another, it's someone who acts like one thing when in reality they are something else. God sees beyond our masks. Most people use hypocritical behavior as an excuse not to go to church—they say stuff like, "That's why I don't go to church—too many hypocrites" and "None of those people are any good." But that's ridiculous because you work with some people who aren't any good but you don't quit your job; you live with some people who aren't any good, but you don't move out of your house, but anyway, that's another subject for another Sunday.

Next, Jesus says that prayer is not about a multitude of words because God is not hearing impaired and God cannot be impressed—at least not with words. In those days, almost like these days, people loved attention. Some people loved to make prayer a public spectacle. Jesus warns against this by saying that we should never pray to be seen, but we should be seen praying, so He gives what has become known as the Lord's Prayer. Now, please note that I disagree with that because it should have been the disciple's prayer because there was some stuff in the prayer Jesus couldn't use for Himself. For instance, He couldn't have said "our Father" because He would have been talking to Himself, and the Bible teaches that Jesus said on more than one occasion, "My Father and I are as one." He couldn't have used "thy kingdom come" because He was the king that had already come. He couldn't have used "forgive us our trespasses" because He knew no sin. He couldn't have used "lead us not into temptation or deliver us from evil" because He was always in control, He gives them a recipe for prayer.

> [9] After this manner therefore pray you: Our Father which art in heaven, Hallowed be thy name.
>
> [10] Thy kingdom come. Thy will be done in earth, as *it is* in heaven.
>
> [11] Give us this day our daily bread.
>
> [12] And forgive us our debts, as we forgive our debtors.
>
> [13] And lead us not into temptation, but deliver us from evil: For thine is the kingdom, and the power, and the glory, forever. Amen.
>
> Matthew 6:9–13 (KJV)

He says, "When you pray, these are the main ingredients." He says, "When you pray, say, Our Father." Notice none of the pronouns in the prayer are singular but are all plural, suggesting that prayer should never be only about our own needs, but to remember your neighbors and brothers and fellow man. So, you see no personal pronouns—only plural pronouns such as "our" and "us." I'm so glad because some folks think nobody knows God but them. Remember, He's our Father, and that includes the person addicted to porn and the prostitute on the strip. He's just as much their Father as He is yours and mine. He's our Father.

Next He says, "Request thy kingdom come." "Kingdom" is a compound word. You remember in school that they taught us that compound words are the coming together of two words to express duality of meaning with singularity of concept. "King" is short for "God," and "dom" is short for "dominion," which means "way of doing things." Put it all together, and you've got "God's way of doing things." He's saying, in essence, that God wants earth to reflect Heaven. There is no greed, murder, envy, disease, jealousy, poverty, or anything like that going on in Heaven. So He said, "Pray God's way of doing things would invade earth." Then He says, "Give us this day our daily bread." I honestly believe He does this because he knows our nature to get selective amnesia and get so wrapped up in the blessing and forget about the Blessor. Just like today, people are humble as long as they need you, and they forget your number when they get up on their feet. So if He gives me today's bread, He knows I'll have to come back for tomorrow's bread. Then He brings up something we struggle with—forgiveness—but look at how He connects the cycle and circle. Forgive us as we forgive. You see, girlfriend, you can't make any demands on God until you are willing to follow some commands as it relates to our human relationships. He made the terms interchangeable. In other words, I want your forgiveness, but I'm also willing to give what I am in the need of. The word "forgive" means to give like you did before. We so often want forgiveness from God, yet we want to hold on to grudges toward others. As we say, we can dish it, but we can't take it.

A story is told of a little girl who was fighting with her big brother, and their father came in and caught them. He said, "I refuse to have my children fighting. I love you both."

The little girl ran and jumped up in her father's arms and hugged his neck and said, "Oh, Daddy, I am so sorry for fighting with my brother. Please forgive me."

It melted her father's heart, and he thought, *Oh, some of my teaching must have rubbed off on my little girl*, but he looked out of the corner of his eye and noticed she was hugging him and sticking her tongue out at her brother at the same time. Her father put her down and said, "No, my daughter, it's impossible to hug daddy around the neck and stick your tongue out at your brother at the same time." So he chastised her and made her go hug her brother.

And that's the way it is with us. We want to hug God around the neck and stick our tongues out at our brothers and sisters, and the two are not synonymous. For He declares, "how can you love God, whom you have never seen, and hate your brother, whom you see daily?"

Then He says, "Lead us not into temptation, but deliver us from evil." When I was younger, I used to think temptation and evil were one and the same. However, I discovered that they were cousins and not siblings. You see, temptation has to do with weakness, whereas evil has to do with wickedness, but these topics themselves are potentially a book on their own, let me just say that temptation is when it overtakes you. Evil is when you overtake it. We all have the tendencies to be both weak at times and wicked.

And don't forget the "Amen," which means "It is so." Yes, this prayer started laid out like a letter. It was written to Our Father, it was addressed to "which art in Heaven." The body was about a will, some bread, some guarding and guiding, and, yes, forgiveness. The postscript was the kingdom, power, and glory. And the stamp on it is the amen.

Don't forget the amen. Amen is like the endorsement on a check. The money can be in the account, and the payee can have proper ID, but the bank won't cash it unless it's been signed. There are four types of amens. There is the amen of expectation, the amen of affirmation, the amen of confirmation, and then the amen of celebration. Affirmation means you believe it. Expectation says you're waiting to receive it. Confirmation means it's so because he said it and that you believe it and will stand on His promise until it becomes manifested on the premise, and celebration means I'll praise Him in advance because it's already done. Prayer is always in order.

Practicality

In this generation, we have raised up society where the spirit of entitlement runs as rampant as a pack of stray dogs in the streets of New York City. This spirit, to those of you who were born before the '70s, is referred to as "spoiled." It's a dangerous spirit. It's one that says boldly, "I want what I want, and I deserve it, whether or not my behavior is deemed reflective of my desire." Oh, yes, it is a dangerous spirit. Entitlement says reward without requirement. It says privilege without pay, and that's the language of most of the population. "You owe me!" they scream at the tops of their lungs. Well, when I was in elementary school, I remember learning about reciprocals, which were the opposite of whatever the compound was, so if the original compound was 2/3, the reciprocal was 3/2; they were opposite and reflective of each other. That is the way relationships should be—opposite yet the same. However, you should be willing to be reflective and reciprocate the effort, zeal, care, and love of your partner and what he or she brings to the equation. No, I'm not saying to the extreme, but as a rule of thumb of sorts, we should never ask of anyone what we are not willing to sacrifice—at least what is equally deserved. I want to say something about practicality as it relates to our desires. Why is that you would want a man or significant other with A-1 credit when your credit can't get you a piece of free bubble gum? Why would you want someone who is in great health and built like a Greek god when you're built like a gummy bear and you act as if you are allergic to exercise? Why would you want someone with character and integrity when every word you say is a lie?

All I am saying is that we all need to do some self-inspections every now and then and make sure we can facilitate what we feel we desire or deserve in companionship. It is unfair for you to bring a person down. As they say, never date or marry down. Yes, that's true, but I also believe the greater virtue is being true to yourself and knowing how to set the bar and raise the standard of our own expectations; therefore, being practical is more about being truthful to oneself and others. Allow me to say there's nothing wrong with wanting better and greater, but can you reciprocate or facilitate what it is you are wanting? Because other people have needs, as well. My aunt Martha said something years ago before she went on to be with the Lord—she used to say it, and she actually wrote it on a card that she presented to me at my high school baccalaureate service. It simply was this: "Charles Edward, the largest room in the world is the room for improvement, and we all have room for that."

Don't be overbearing, overcritical, or over judgmental of yourself; however, be truthful, and work on the areas that you know or at least think that you could improve on. I say this because the sad reality is most people don't understand that you will never marry perfection. At best, you will marry potential. Not that it won't be sickness and health, better and worse, but let's not start off in sickness and at worse.

Preparation the Final Frontier

I have heard it said many times that success is when opportunity and preparation kiss. The only problem is that some people are prepared and don't get the opportunity, and some people sadly get the opportunity and are not prepared.

Whichever the case, never underestimate preparation. In order to know your calling and to whom and what you are called to, is to also understand that each of us in order to be fulfilled have to be a part of something bigger than ourselves; yet, being prepared is oftentimes overlooked. In many cases, we have fairytale images of what we perceive a thing is supposed to look like, thus leaving us with a sense of disappointment when our expectations are not met. Being prepared either way is a rule of thumb that one should always be mindful of. I call this managing your own expectations— not dumbing down or refusing to dream or reach for the stars but preparing yourself so that you understand how to make the necessary adjustments for life's little incidentals. I have a wonderful team and staff at New Wine Church International, and I'm willing to put them up against the best, but I am also mindful of what Dr. I. V. Hilliard said in a conference I attended at his church in Houston, Texas. He spoke of how when the Lord was leading him to change his preaching style and make some changes and adjustments in his worship style, almost 80 percent of his congregation got up and walked out one Sunday and he said to those of us as pastors, "You've got to know what to do if one Sunday everybody in your church decides not to show up or abandons you." That resonated with me, and although I love my media team and I make sure they have proper training and adequate tools to perform their ministry with, I am still prepared to run the cameras if I have to or until I can replace them.

Call it a proverbial plan B or a spare tire— that's your choice, but be prepared, and so that I won't sound cynical, negative, or pessimistic, prepare for the best, as well. Yes, by all means, prepare yourself so that you can be proud of what value you add. You are an answer and a problem solver for someone or something on this planet. Yes, you may be multigifted, talented, and knowledgeable in several areas and fields; however, be prepared in areas also that you lack or are deficient in, because knowing your CUP size is also about stretching yourself so that you can be not just average or subpar but so that you may say when the light shines on you that you were born for the part. If you want to be married and you can't cook, get prepared by at least taking a cooking class. Even if he can cook, be prepared, for if something were to happen and he's late getting in from work, are you and the kids supposed to always do takeout or sit there and starve until daddy arrives? Prepare your temple. If you know you need to work on some health issues that are within your control, prepare by changing your diet and positioning yourself to present your mate with a healthy bride and not a basketful of health challenges. Again, yes, I know the vows say in sickness and in health, but at least try to not start off that way.

Be prepared. Again, I repeat that God does not always give you what you pray for, but he gives you what you are prepared for. Why would God give you a mansion when your apartment is nasty and unclean? Why would he give you a Mercedes when your hoopty stays dirty and unwashed or uncared for? Why would he give you a husband when you can't keep a boyfriend? No, I am not saying that we men don't have our own sets of issues; trust and believe that I'm going to check them in *CUP Size Matters for Men* (coming soon—just a little free commercial); however, I just want to speak to you, my sister, so that you will have a reality check and vantage point over and above those who are still looking through rose-colored glasses. Be prepared. As Bishop Jakes would say, "Get ready, get ready, get ready, get ready. And if you're ready, stay ready, stay ready, stay ready."

He are some things that will help you better understand your calling.

> There is victory in your vocal cords, so make these following confessions a part of your daily confessions.
>
> I *will* embrace my current season of life and live with the spirit of contentment.

6 Yet true godliness with contentment is itself great wealth.

1 Timothy 6:6 (NLT)

I *will* champion God's model for womanhood and teach it to my children.

4 No, your beauty should come from within you—the beauty of a gentle and quiet spirit that will never be destroyed and is very precious to God.

1 Peter 3:4 (NCV)

I *will* embrace my God-given uniqueness and celebrate the distinctions He has placed in others.

5 "I knew you before I formed you in your mother's womb. Before you were born I set you apart and appointed you as my prophet to the nations."

Jeremiah 1:5 (NLT)

I *will* live as a woman answerable to God and faithfully committed to His Word.

14 I have rejoiced in your laws as much as in riches.

15 I will study your commandments and reflect on your ways.

16 I will delight in your decrees and not forget your word.

Psalms 119:14–16 (NLT)

I *will* seek to devote the best of myself to the primary roles God has entrusted to me.

17 And whatever you do, whether in word or deed, do it all in the name of the Lord Jesus, giving thanks to God the Father through him.

Colossians 3:17 (NIV)

I *will* be quick to listen, slow to speak, and esteem others more highly than myself.

3 Don't be selfish; don't try to impress others. Be humble, thinking of others as better than yourselves.

⁴ Don't look out only for your own interests, but take an interest in others, too.

Philippians 2:3–4 (NLT)

I *will* forgive those who have wronged me and reconcile with those I have wronged.

¹³ Make allowance for each other's faults, and forgive anyone who offends you. Remember, the Lord forgave you, so you must forgive others.

Colossians 3:13 (NLT)

I *will not* tolerate evil influences in myself or my home but will embrace a life of purity.

² I will be careful to live a blameless life— when will you come to help me? I will lead a life of integrity in my own home.

Psalms 101:2 (NLT)

I *will* pursue justice, love mercy, and extend compassion toward others.

⁸ He has showed you, O man, what is good. And what does the LORD require of you? To act justly and to love mercy and to walk humbly with your God.

Micah 6:8 (NIV)

I *will* be faithful to my husband and honor him in my conduct and in my conversation, and I will aspire to be a suitable partner to help him reach his God-given potential.

⁴ An excellent wife is the crown of her husband, But she who shames *him* is like rottenness in his bones.

Proverbs 12:4 (NASB)

I *will* teach my children to love God, respect authority, and live responsibly.

⁶ These commandments that I give you today are to be upon your hearts.

⁷ Impress them on your children. Talk about them when you sit at home and when you walk along the road, when you lie down and when you get up.

Deuteronomy 6:6-7 (NIV)

I *will* cultivate a peaceful home where God's presence is sensed.

¹ A gentle answer turns away wrath, but a harsh word stirs up anger.

Proverbs 15:1 (NIV)

I *will* make today's decisions with tomorrow's impact in mind and consider my current choices in light of future generations.

¹⁶ I command you today to love the LORD your God, to walk in His ways and to keep His commandments and His statutes and His judgments, that you may live and multiply, and that the LORD your God may bless you in the land where you are entering to possess it. So choose life in order that you may live, you and your descendants.

Deuteronomy 30:16,19 (NASB)

I *will* courageously work with the strength God provides to fulfill this resolution for the rest of my life and for His glory.

¹³ I have strength for all things in Christ Who empowers me [I am ready for anything and equal to anything through Him Who infuses inner strength into me; I am self-sufficient in Christ's sufficiency].

Philippians 4:13 (AMP)

¹³ Whatever I have, wherever I am, I can make it through anything in the One who makes me who I am.

Philippians 4:13 (MSG)

Knowing your CUP size begins with knowing what the *C* stands for, and the *C* stands for "**Calling**"!

CHAPTER 5

The U Stands for _ _ _ _ _ _ _ _ _ _

The *U* stands for "uniqueness." Yes, you are indeed an original. If I could get every woman to see that she is unique, what a world we would have.

Girlfriend, it's alright to pattern, model, admire, and follow in the footsteps of the wonderful women you admire and look up to or who blazed the trail before you, but always remember that imitation can also mean limitation. You are so you unique that you have absolutely no competition at being you. If someone were going to be just like you, they would have to have been conceived at the very same millisecond as you in the same bed by the same parents in the same room in the same city at the same time and get the same set of twenty-three chromosomes from your father, and at best she would only be a twin. Plainly put, someone else could never be you. You are so unique that even if we tried to clone you, it would only be at best a close resemblance. But you, my sista, are *unique*.

Having said that, welcome to the campus of "U" University, where you will be majoring in U-ology with a minor in I-matter.

Do You See What I See?

Images are needful. The etymology of the word "imagine" or "image" comes from the midfourteenth century "to form a mental image of," from the Old French word *imaginer*, *meaning to* "sculpt, carve, paint; decorate, embellish," which derived from the thirteenth century, from Latin *imaginari*, "to form a mental picture to oneself."

I love the Latin, which says "to form a mental picture to oneself," not of oneself but to oneself. I wanted to hone in on this word because images play such an important role in how our everyday lives play out, from how we treat ourselves to how we are treated by others. We normally buy into the images that society sells us or paints as being acceptable pretty, ugly, cool, or uncool, but the first letter in the word image is *I*, and *I* counts for so much.

You must begin to understand that you are only as great as your willingness to begin to embrace your uniqueness. It is at the point that you wholly realize that you truly have no competition at being you. Then you get the revelation that you really were created to celebrate your individualism, even in a collective culture.

Now, please don't take offense. I know that you can Google words that you care to or want the definition of, so this is no attempt to reprint an abridged dictionary, but pay attention to the following definition of the word "unique" because I feel if we understand a thing at its root, then we can understand what is meant by it. I say this because sometimes I believe this generation confuses uniqueness with being bizarre and awkward looking, and therefore they go to extremes with hairstyles and clothes, which is okay if that's what you like, but sometimes that doesn't say *I'm unique*; it really says *I'm desperate for attention*, so I want, for the book's sake, to be clear:

> The word unique is an adjective derived c.1600, "single, solitary," from French *unique*, from Latin *unicus* "single, sole," from *unus* "one" (see). Meaning "forming the only one of its kind" is attested from 1610s; erroneous sense of "remarkable, uncommon" is attested from mid-19c. uni means one u·nique yu nik [yoo-neek] *adjective:*
>
> 1. existing as the only one or as the sole example; single; solitary in type or characteristics: *a unique copy of an ancient manuscript.*
>
> 2. having no like or equal; unparalleled; incomparable: *Bach was unique in his handling of counterpoint.*
>
> 3. not typical; unusual: *She has a very unique smile. (Definitions are from dictionary.com)*

Just by mere definition, we see the word itself gives off the aroma of being in a class by itself; likewise, we are the same. Although there are several people I admire, I still have to uniquely be myself. Yes, we are in the same boat, yet we all paddle differently.

Whoever tries cannot equal up to you. There will never be another George Washington, Thomas Jefferson, Dr. Martin Luther King Jr., Fannie Lou Hamer, Joan of Arc, Mary Magdalene, or Dr. Charles Pepper, the inventor of the soft drink known today as Dr. Pepper, patented in 1906 by the Dr. Pepper Co. in Dallas, Texas, named for US physician Dr. Charles Pepper. Imagine if he tried to be Coca-Cola. All I am saying is that you are unique.

You Are Not a Universal Remote

Now allow me to show you something. One time, I purchased a television and somehow—I don't quiet remember how, I lost or damaged the remote that came with it, but they had come out with these universal remotes. Problem solved, right? I wish it were only that easy. I went and purchased a universal remote (a remote that supposedly works with most brands of televisions). I had to program it and find the code on my TV that matched, and at the end of the day, I hated it. I mean, it worked, but it was nothing like the one that came with the TV.

You are a unique woman, not a universal remote control. You were not designed to work with any brand or just anybody. Look at the definition of universal.

u·ni·ver·sal

yun   v rs l [yoo-n*uh*-vur-s*uhl*] *adjective*

1. of, pertaining to, <u>or</u> characteristic of all or the whole: *universal experience.*

2. applicable everywhere or in all cases; general: *a universal cure.*

3. affecting, concerning, or involving all: *universal military service.*

4. used or understood by all: *a universal <u>language</u>.*

5. present everywhere: *the universal calm of southern seas. (All definitions were collected from dictionary.com)*

Some people like trying to be every woman and all things to all people, but that's so blah. How would we differentiate or separate? Everyone would get you confused.

John Mason, best-selling author of *An Enemy Called Average*, tells in one of his books the story of a middle-aged woman who had a heart attack. She was rushed to the emergency room, and on the operating table, she had a near-death experience. Seeing God, she asked if this was it. He said, "No, you have another forty-three years, two months, and eight days to live." Upon recovery, she decided to stay in the hospital and have a face-lift, tummy tuck, liposuction—the whole works. She had someone come in and change her hair color, figuring that since she had so much life to live, she might as well make the most of it.

She was discharged following the final procedure; however, while crossing the street outside, she was killed by a speeding ambulance.

Arriving in God's presence, she fumed, "I thought you said I had another forty-plus years."

He replied, "I didn't recognize you."

She traded in the only thing she had original which was her uniqueness. I am spending this whole section of the book to hammer home one point— you are the apple of God's eye the way that He made you. I admire lots of people, but I would rather be a good original than a great copy. In school, we used to hate copycats. Now, also let me say there is nothing wrong with being a copycat as long as you copy the right cat. A Congolese proverb states that wood may remain in water for ten years, but it will never become a crocodile.

Jeremiah 13:23 (KJV) says, "Can the Ethiopian change his skin, or the leopard his spots?"

You are an original, but the first key to wisdom is calling a thing by its correct name. When people don't recognize their uniqueness, they constantly adjust themselves to try to fit into everybody's box. They buy clothes that don't fit and get hairstyles that look good on other people. It is such a waste of energy. Dare to be who you are and make your own impression in life.

Consider these words from one of history's greatest artists:

> My mother said to me, "If you become a soldier, you'll become a general; if you become a monk, you'll end up as pope." Instead, I became a painter and ended up Picasso.

Yes, my sista, there will be disappointments, faults, flaws, and failures, but stop making excuses to not be you. Knowing your CUP size is also accepting the fact that you are not perfect, but you are being perfected.

> I've missed more than 9,000 shots in my career. I've lost almost 300 games. Twenty-six times I've been trusted to take the game winning shot ... and missed. I have failed over, and over, and over again in my life. That's why I succeed.
>
> —Michael Jordan (arguably the greatest basketball player ever)

Stop building a case against yourself. Stop finding reasons to say why not. Success was built in cans and not cant's. The biggest successes are the people who solve the biggest problems. Problems are the price of progress.

Thomas Edison was afraid of the dark, but he was the unique individual who invented the lightbulb. Sometimes you must be willing to look inside of your fears and inhibitions to find that one thing that you can do that no one else on earth was called to do.

Now, allow me to say something relational. You may know your uniqueness but also know that knowing your CUP size entails some tailoring; however, sometimes that uniqueness is blindsided because you have spent so much time neglecting your race by trying to run in someone else's lane.

The writer of Hebrews points this out so vividly:

> ¹ Wherefore seeing we also are compassed about with so great a cloud of witnesses, let us lay aside every weight, and the sin which doth so easily beset *us*, and let us run with patience the race that is set before us,
>
> ² Looking unto Jesus the author and finisher of *our* faith; who for the joy that was set before him endured the cross, despising the shame, and is set down at the right hand of the throne of God.
>
> Hebrews 12:1–2 (KJV)

The race that is set before us catches my attention because the Hebrew writer points out first our individuality. Although there are several runners, each must stay in his or her own lanes, subsequently running the race that is set before them. Wow!

The writer of the book of Hebrews views life as a race. It's viewed as a race that you are in whether you want to be in it or not. Strangely enough, the word "race" has many derivatives, but at its root, it means to go or to move, but it also carries the idea of conflict. It also carries the connotation of struggle. In this life, whether you want to be in it or not, you are involved in some kind of struggle, and this is a race that is set before us, meaning you can't forego it because it was set before us or before our arrival.

There are some things you have no choice about. For instance, you didn't choose your height or your color, the width of your nose, the color of your hair, or the color of your eyes. You had nothing to do with that. You didn't choose how long you would live or how short you would live or whether your parents would have money or be broke. You didn't choose whether you would be black or white. There was no choice; it was set before us. You didn't choose your gifts or your talents. I mean, if we could, we would all go to the store and buy some vocal cords like Justin Timberlake, Michael Jackson, or Aretha Franklin. Or we would all have tip-top physiques like Usher or Billy Blanks or a body like Kim Kardashian, Heidi Klum, or Venus and Serena Williams.

I'm saying whatever you have, you didn't order it. It was your lot because your race is set. In this race, you do not choose your difficulties or your challenges because sometimes the race chooses you. Dr. Martin Luther King Jr. told the story of how he was chosen as the leader of the civil rights movement after Mrs. Rosa Parks wouldn't give up her seat on a bus to a white man and was thrown in jail. The churches got together to form the Montgomery Improvement Association to boycott the bus system and they needed somebody with a clean record. The only one they could find was this young minister fresh out of Morehouse College named Martin Luther King Jr. All I'm saying is he didn't choose it. It chose him because that was the race that was set before him. So,unique to our own existence. It is during these unique moments while in your race that knowing your CUP size will help you better recognize life's defining moments.

You are so unique that no one can handle your unique set of circumstances like you do. No one will have the patience with that child like you do. Other people would have given up on your marriage, but you're equipped to deal with that wayward spouse. Embrace your uniqueness to the point that you never waste a good storm, because only you can deal with it in a way no one else can.

A story is told of a man who had a son who was in and out of trouble. The son would go to jail, and every time, the father would go bail him out. It seemed as though every time you turned around, the man had to go get his son out of jail. His friend said to him one day, "Man, if that were my boy, I wouldn't go get him this time. He needs to learn a lesson." The gentleman whose son was in jail said, "If he were your boy, I wouldn't go get him, either, but he's my son, and I'm going to get him." God has given you a grace to handle your unique situation that others don't understand and no doubt would have given up on.

There are others who did not choose their races. For instance, there are those who were born blind or born handicapped and some of them were born in poverty. Some of their parents gave them up. Some had all kinds of problems, disadvantages, and bad situations. Some people have money. Some people don't have money. Some people are barren. Some people have children by the busloads. They are like the old lady in the shoe who had so many children that she didn't know what to do. But this race, believe me when I tell you, it's been set.

There are different types of races, there are some sprints, there are some marathons, and some long-distance runs. And let me say this when someone dies young it's hard for us to make sense out of why his or her life was cut short, but that life was like a sprint, and people who live a long time, their race is like a marathon, but your race is set.

And since the race is set, there are some things in which you don't have a choice and some things in which you do have a choice. You have a choice of who is going to be with you and who your Savior is going to be while on this race. It's good to have Jesus with you on this race, because you were chosen before the foundation of the world. God had a plan for your life before He had a plan for the world, and then He says in Psalms that our steps have been ordered. I'm simply trying to say to you that you don't have to worry about the race when you have Jesus running alongside you. He will help you run this race that is set before us.

I May Be Unique, but I Am Not My Mistake!

The writer of that same passage also says that there is a cloud or a crowd of witnesses in chapter 12, although he is referring to what is called the hall of faith of the Bible in Hebrews 11. More so, they are named, and these witnesses provide us examples and inspirations because the witnesses had all kinds of unique problems, difficulties, issues and situations, and yet they ran their races successfully.

Noah was the first shipbuilder and preached for 120 years, and only eight people were saved. Noah had a chemical-dependency problem, and God still used him. Noah made the cut, and that's inspiration.

Abraham was known as God's friend, the father of the faithful, and yet Abraham had a pimp spirit, for he allowed his wife to participate in swinging with the king to make their lives easier, and he lied and said that Sarah was his sister and not his wife, but God still used him. That's inspiration.

Moses is mentioned here in the hall of faith. You remember Pastor Moses, don't you? He was the one who killed an Egyptian and buried him in the sand, and yet he made it.

And consider David, the sweet singer of Israel—you know, the one who wrote, "The Lord is my shepherd," and "The Lord is my light and my salvation whom shall I fear and of whom shall I be afraid." I don't know if he was a voyeur or an exhibitionist, but he was up on the roof and watched another man's wife sunbathe and got her pregnant and then had her husband killed to cover it up (and you thought *Scandal* was a nail-biter) yet he was called a man after God's own heart. If David made it to the hall of fame of faith, then certainly there's hope for you and me.

The hall of fame of faith mentions Samson. You remember Samson, don't you? His own momma and daddy came to him and said, "You know what, son? You have a penchant for this Philistine woman. Why can't you get you a nice Hebrew girl?" Samson said, (and let me give you the Charles Bond version), "But those foreign girls, they please me. Their milk shakes bring all the boys to the yard." As one of our recent hip-hop artists just put out in a song, he says, "Just help me get one." And yet even though Samson got his hair cut in the wrong barbershop, Samson made it.

I hear you saying, "You didn't mention any women." Well, there is Rahab the prostitute, and she had the best little whorehouse in Egypt. Oh, you heard about the red-light district. Well, maybe it started with Rahab when she would let down a red cord or rope out the window so that when the soldiers would return, they would not kill her or her family. And you would ask, "Why would God put her in the hall of faith and in the heroes' hall of fame?" And yet Rahab was in the lineage of Jesus … and she made it.

It seems like God is saying that you can be the lowest of the low and commit your sin over and over and over again. You can be caught in a mess you ain't got no business in, and yet He can take you and place you in the lineage of Jesus Christ, and it seems to suggest that no matter what you've been caught up in and no matter what you're in now, God has your race set before you. These individuals were all unique in their situations and their sins. I just want you to take away one thing from these examples, and that is *you are not your mistake*! In spite of all that these individuals did, they were known for their faith; not their flaws, faults, and failures.

Repeat This Ten Times: I Am Not My Mistake!

Not only do we learn that each of them was unique in their situations and that their sins were unique, we learn that the Creator used them all. The point of that rhetoric was not to air out our favorite biblical characters' dirty laundry as to give out license not to strive for moral rectitude; but, rather to say that we are in great company in spite of our own unique fallacies and God can still use us.

Next We See Not Only Inspiration but Instructions

Unique people always have a different way of doing things, but truth be told, sometimes it's just best to follow the instructions. The writer says, "Let us lay aside every weight and sin that doth so easily beset us or throws us off and hinders our progress." The original language for the word "weight" is the Greek word "oncos" It's where we get our English word "oncology." It's a mass or growth, which we know in worst-case scenarios leads to cancer, depending upon whether it is malignant or benign.

The writer says that there are some weighty things that, if not discarded, dealt with, or done away with, could potentially grow into something that could become detrimental. You see, in those days, runners ran naked as to not be hindered by any form of distractions. That would have made for a heck of an Olympic commercial! But on a serious note, it showed their determination not to allow anything to distract, take away from, or to stand in their way. I want to speak about that because you are unique and have a race that is set before you, and it's imperative that you strip away people problems and toxic relationships that may trip you up. It may be an attitude or it could be a negative disposition, and you may need counseling, but whatever you have to do, please get rid of the "oncos." It may start small, but if you don't deal with it before it deals with you, then that uniqueness will die before its time. And please don't let it overwhelm you. He's in the race with you, and whatever is over your head, it's still under His feet.

Now This Uniqueness Required a Trailblazer

You have an example, because, for unique people, you would feel awkward or very reclusive and lonely if you thought you were alone with no example. There always has to be a trailblazer. I mean, think about it. The Jackson family was loaded with talent, but there was something a little bit more unique about Michael. The Osmond family was as diversely gifted and talented as any family on earth, but Donnie and Marie were chosen to stand out front and represent the family. That is not at all to suggest that the other children in both of these families were any less; however, there is always that one unique individual that shines a little brighter.

Knowing your CUP size and your uniqueness comes with a downside. It makes you an easier target because you are out front. But you are in great company, and never dumb down or downplay your uniqueness because of other people's insecurities or nonacceptance. I heard the great Dr. Cindy Trimm say, "You should never have to stop being who you are because someone is intimidated by your anointing." Dr. W. J. Dixon III once said, "Confidence is normally looked at as arrogance by people who don't have any."

Again, being unique places you in great company. Look at Jesus there was no one like Him, so much so that no one was ever born like him, and although some may have died on a cross, all that died like Him still remain in the grave, they didn't get up like Him.

There's nobody like Jesus. Who would have ever known anything about a manger in Bethlehem if Jesus had not been born there? Who would have ever known anything about a little town called Nazareth if Jesus had not come from there, or about the Sea of Galilee if He had not sailed there, about the pool of Bethesda if He had not healed there, about Jacob's well if He had not sat there, about Calvary if He had not died there, and about Joseph's new tomb if He had not been buried there? Just his uniqueness alone put all of these places and things in history because He was there.

Need Further Evidence

Jesus was so unique that one day, someone asked Him, "Jesus, how old are you?" He answered, "Well, it depends on whose side you're talking about. On my mother's side, they say I was born in a manger. On my daddy's side, I was from in the beginning. On my momma's side, I'm twelve, but on my daddy's side, I'm older than time because I'm from everlasting to everlasting. On my mother's side, I swung on vines; on daddy's side, I am the true vine. On momma's side, I smelled lilies and roses, and on my daddy's side, I am the lily of the valley and the rose of Sharon. On my momma's side, I drank wine, but on my daddy's side, I turned water into wine. On my momma's side, I used to look up at the stars, but on my daddy's side, I am the bright and morning star. On my momma's side, I ate bread, but on my daddy's side, I am the bread of life. On my momma's side, I used to play in the rain, but on my daddy's side, I stood on a ship one day and calmed the storm by saying, "Peace. Be still." On my momma's side, I used go get water from the well, but on my daddy's side, I went to a well one day to meet the woman of Samaria, and I sat on the well, and it was a well sitting on a well because in me was living water and the water of life. On my momma's side, I would eat fish, but on my daddy's side, I made my disciples fishers of men."

Your Uniqueness Allows You to Handle Haters

Now, understand that being unique doesn't mean that everybody's going to like you and be in your corner pulling for you. Being unique will cause you to have some enemies, and it may not be folks across the room that stab you in the back, it may be those close to you, because they were the ones who got close enough to know where to put the knife. You see, you may be the dog's bowwow and the cat's meow but sometimes success breeds enemies, even in your own family. You remember Joseph, don't you? Well, Joseph was a dreamer and the Bible says this:

> 2 These *are* the generations of Jacob. Joseph, *being* seventeen years old, was feeding the flock with his brethren; and the lad *was* with the sons of Bilhah, and with the sons of Zilpah, his father's wives: and Joseph brought unto his father their evil report.

> 3 Now Israel loved Joseph more than all his children, because he *was* the son of his old age: and he made him a coat of *many* colours.

> 4 And when his brethren saw that their father loved him more than all his brethren, they hated him, and could not speak peaceably unto him.

> 5 And Joseph dreamed a dream, and he told *it* his brethren: and they hated him yet the more.

> 6 And he said unto them, Hear, I pray you, this dream which I have dreamed:

> 7 For, behold, we *were* binding sheaves in the field, and, lo, my sheaf arose, and also stood upright; and, behold, your sheaves stood round about, and made obeisance to my sheaf.

> 8 And his brethren said to him, Shalt thou indeed reign over us? or shalt thou indeed have dominion over us? And they hated him yet the more for his dreams, and for his words.

> 9 And he dreamed yet another dream, and told it his brethren, and said, Behold, I have dreamed a dream more; and, behold, the sun and the moon and the eleven stars made obeisance to me.

¹⁰ And he told *it* to his father, and to his brethren: and his father rebuked him, and said unto him, What *is* this dream that thou hast dreamed? Shall I and thy mother and thy brethren indeed come to bow down ourselves to thee to the earth?

¹¹ And his brethren envied him; but his father observed the saying.

Genesis 37:2–11 (KJV)

Wow. Joseph was a dreamer, and you would think his family would get behind the vision, right? Wrong. They got jealous and decided that they would be envious. Yes, his brothers—not the kids from the neighborhood, but those who shared his same gene pool and anatomical makeup. Yes, his brothers, who later would scheme up a plan that they would steal the coat his father had made and dip it in blood and tell their father a wild beast devoured him and that they buried him in a well, but instead sold him to a band of Midianites. He would later end up in jail for a crime he didn't commit and be in prison, but the Bible says the Lord was with him. From the pit to the palace, he had favor—so much so that he ended up becoming the governor and was placed over the welfare department and issued the food stamps when a famine came—if you will allow me to use my spiritual imagination and put it in contemporary terms. And guess who needed to eat when things got tough? His brothers. They had to come to Joseph for help. They eventually found out who he was, but initially, they didn't recognize him, but Joseph didn't rub it in their faces, he just told them thank you because they thought they were putting him down when really, they were propelling him to his destiny. They stole his coat, but they couldn't steal his favor Lastly, we learn from this story that God will make your enemies your employees and when people don't recognize you, sometimes it's because they haven't grown, but you have.

Now, I don't totally blame his brothers, because although Joseph had the dreams, his judgment was bad. He tried to share private information too soon. Again I say, don't be surprised when even your own family does not receive you because you are unique. So it was with Jesus. His own family, the church of that day, didn't receive Jesus because He wasn't trying to fit in. He was unique, and subsequently, that led to His death. For the Bible says, "Yet he came to his own, and they received him not." I'm still amazed that gangs and thugs and sinners did not kill Jesus. It was religious folks, and they resented Him and even crucified Him because He was—you guessed it—*unique.* So you see, girlfriend, uniqueness can be a blessed curse. If not Him, then who? If not you, then who?. Let me close this chapter with this;

The writer of Hebrews said this: "looking unto Jesus the Author and finisher of our faith." Look at the word "author" there. In the original Greek, it's the word "arkhaygos," which is translated "first leader." It's derived from the culture of that day when ships would set out to sail with their passengers. Whenever they arrived close to the shore, the ship could not get in too close because they were not as advanced as we are now, so they had a system. What they would do is find the fastest, strongest, best swimmer and tie a rope around him, and he would jump into the stormy, choppy, wavy water and swim to shore and tie his end of the rope to a tree. Then those who could not swim so well or even at all, could make it into shore by holding on to the rope. Well, Jesus was our "arkhaygos." He tackled life and death like no other. He was unique, and because He conquered it first, those of us who are unique can live out loud because we have an "arkhaygos" as an example of what a trailblazer and unique prototype looks like.

Embracing Your Uniqueness Will Cause You To Do Some U_ _ _ _ _ _ _ _ _ _ _ (Underwriting)!

Some underwriting is required as you learn your CUP size. You are not only unique in and of yourself; you are also unique for someone else. We often waste time in dead-end relationships because we do not do what the Greeks call "hupogrammos," which is underwriting. It's the process banks use to research your credit and lifestyle in order to determine if you are a good risk or not before they loan you money. The same happens with insurance companies. If banks in a worldly system and insurance companies of the world do proper investigation to see if you pass underwriting or are a good risk, what about you and me? We should do our own underwriting, because some people are a bad risk. I have several underwriters who are on my leadership team at New Wine Church International, the church where I am fortunate enough to serve as lead pastor. They share with me—without of course disclosing anyone's personal or private business—that they have to turn people down often or deny loans and claims because the individual could not pass underwriting or were deemed as a risk for a loan.

Now, don't get me wrong, we shouldn't go around putting people through all kinds of rigorous litmus tests, knowing we don't have what we are asking of them. I mean, why are you asking for someone to be your life mate when they have a stellar reputation and your reputation is of ill repute, or vice versa? Why would you allow someone who is irresponsible to mess up your credibility? I often say that you can't allow someone to come in and tear down in twenty months what it took you twenty years to build up. This is beyond visual. As a woman who may be in the market for a suitable mate, before you commit to someone your uniqueness, you should do your underwriting and see if that person has what I refer to as the six Cs.

And don't just focus on whether he is attractive. Have you really checked him out? You also must remember to be enough of a open book where if you ask for honesty, you can handle it.

So, every man needs the six Cs. Please note these are just the basics, because you can't build something solid on a shaky foundation.

1. He needs a relationship with *Christ*—he doesn't just go to church but has a relationship with God. If a man can't lead you in worship, he can't lead you anywhere but down.

2. He needs to have *character*. This is determined by his consistency. Does he keep his word, or does he display the habit of always making excuses? And also, what do those who are closest say about him? Example: if his mothers and sisters say he's no good, you might want to pass on this one because they've had time to observe him; you may have just met him on Facebook or a social media dating site.

3. He needs *credibility*, which is his believability. This requires you doing some footwork—don't hire a private detective, but just observe keenly, and don't be blinded by a smoke signal. If he has a job, he ought to have a job ID badge or a current pay stub. In court, they say it's not what is factual but it's what you can prove.

4. He needs to have *cash*. He doesn't have to be one of the Rockefellers or Donald Trump. Plus, you know your CUP size, so you can't be bought even if he is: but remember that *ro*mance without *fi*nance is *ig*norance. Being broke also makes someone a *nui*sance.

5. He needs a *crib*. He needs his own address where he receives his mail. This is a nonnegotiable. A grown man doesn't need to be pillar to post or from one couch to the next, nor does He need to even think he's gonna crash at your place. No. And remember, "No" is a complete sentence.

6. Lastly, he needs a *car*, and I'll work with a brother. Let's say if he can't drive or has a handicap, he needs at least two good bus passes (I told you that I am an equal-opportunity guy).

Now, these checklist items are not the end-all and be-all. There are many things that must be present, like chemistry and attraction. But the underwriting piece is really to cause you to think beyond the surface, because anyone can present a good shell, but it's what's inside the nut once you crack it open that matters.

I want to conclude this section with what I call the ten commandments of knowing the uniqueness of your CUP size. I hope you can handle it.

1. Thou shalt not avoid getting measured. Girlfriend, listen, there is nothing stopping you from taking some time out of your busy schedule, going by the mall (this is a good excuse if you need one—don't tell anyone I told you), go to a store that sells undergarments, like Victoria's Secret, Lane Bryant, Nordstrom, or Macy's, and get measured. You need to know, not guestimate, because the girls are too valuable for assumptions.

2. Thou shalt not ever walk out of your house uncertain of your CUP size another day of your life! Girlfriend, this is serious. While you are running around seeking approval and attention from the world, go shut in, meditate, and get to know who you are for yourself, because if you don't know your CUP size, how do you expect us to know? You live in your body; we don't. You should be the most knowledgeable person on the subject of *you*.

3. Thou shalt be proud of your packaging. This is key in how the world will perceive your CUP-size knowledge. Every mother thinks her baby is the cutest and that her child is the smartest, but even if it's not true, she is convinced. You must get a strong conviction and be converted to the religion called *you*. Not in a self-conceited, arrogant, erudite manner. Yet understand, especially from a male perspective, that we take our cues from the director of the movie. You are the director, so you decide when to cut or when it's time to say *action*.

4. Thou shalt not compare. All right, missy. Remember, you are unique, so if God would have wanted you to be a size 6, you

would not be in a size 16 body, so dress up your size 16, and shake what your momma gave you. Stop looking over the fence and *focus* on the goal in front of you. No more living your life trying to fit in someone else's box. The measure of your success is determined not by what the people around you are doing but if you are living your dreams.

5. Thou shalt not compete. Okay, reality check. Competition is out there, but by all means, they are not you. You possess the secret sauce of being you. No matter how hard the rest try, they will never be you. You've got home-court advantage and your fans are in the stands with all their fan favorites pulling for you every step of the way. Don't let us down!

6. Thou shalt not complain. Yes, I said it, and I mean it. No complaining. The time will never be right. There will never be enough money. There will always be life happening all around you, so take the lemons, run to the grocery store, grab some stevia (or sugar), and go home and make some lemonade. Stop and think about what Dr. Cindy Trimm so eloquently said: "Maybe things are the way they are because you are the way you are." Stop competing, comparing, and complaining, and start conquering.

7. Thou shalt use what you have. I'm preaching to the choir with this one. I used to think, if I had better equipment or more money or adequate tools, that I could do more. However, these are just excuses to stay in Stuckville. You may not be able to afford a gym membership, but walking around the block is free. Can't afford the book you want? A library membership is free. Can't get the latest orange juicer? Squeezing them will strengthen your hand muscles. All I'm saying is use what you have.

8. Thou shalt *not* use negative speech. Repeat after me out loud: "Victory begins in the vocal cords." Now say that out loud until it gets in your spirit. By all means, stop decreeing and declaring negative words in your environment and atmosphere. Remember that if no one else is listening, you still hear yourself, and those negative words breed negative feelings and attract negative thoughts, thus creating negative results. There's nothing wrong with talking to yourself; just don't start talking back to yourself.

9. Thou shalt get a grip on your choices. Never give away your personal power to anyone. Some unknown author once said, "I used to have a handle on life, but it broke." Well, I have come to serve notice—get out the superglue and make some new choices. Life is choice driven. Right now, without knowing your name, I can tell you that everything going on or happening in your life is a result of a choice, whether it was made for you or made by you, in order to achieve the change, adjust the choice. So what if you dropped out of school? They still offer night classes. So what if you had a baby out of wedlock? The people who wrote that rule and had you bound in bondage about it are probably guilty of worse. All I'm saying is change your mind, change your choices, change your situation, and change your life.

10. Thou shalt never show your hand. I saved this one for last on purpose. Listen, you. Yeah, you, the one reading my book. In cards, especially spades and poker, there's a rule: never, ever, ever, ever show your hand. You may not be the hottest pot on the stove, the brightest bulb in the box, or the sharpest knife in the drawer, but they should never know it. If you must cry, go in the bathroom stall and cry a river, and then go back to your cubical and smile like you just got a promotion. God did not give you the spirit of fear but of power, love and a sound mind. Yes, there are going to be some rough days ahead, and yes, the heartaches and heartbreaks of the past are the birthmarks of winners, but just keep going, and your CUP size will prove to them who you are without you saying a word.

CHAPTER 6

Tɧe P stanðs for P _ _ _ _ _ _

The *P* stands for "purpose."

I am not really a shopper, but (here comes another confession) *I love to dress*, and when I do, I often get compliments on how well the outfit or suit is put together or how good I smell. Now I'm not telling you this to sound like I'm intoxicated with myself, but it's a sad dog that won't wag his own tail. People will often ask where I found my shoes or where I got my tie and pocket candy (the handkerchief that's in my suit pocket), and I liberally share because I want all of us to present our best selves; Yet, this provoked me to think one day, what if finding intangible things were that easy? Like, where can I find that confidence like yours, or where did you get that self-esteem, or better yet, where can I find purpose? I wish it were as easy as saying, "Oh, they happen to have some on sale at Bloomingdales or Saks Fifth Avenue. How about I pick you up a bottle of purpose when I go by there on my way home from work?" Truth be told, it's not that simple or Walmart wouldn't be able to keep it on the shelves.

This is, ladies, the most important P in knowing your CUP size— knowing your purpose. Well, here we go with those definitions again, but you need to know what it is before you can know how to find it.

Definition of purpose (n)

reason for existence: the reason for which something exists or for which it has been done or made or created , used, etc. an intended or desired result; end; aim; <u>goal</u>. determination; resoluteness. the subject in hand; the point at issue. practical result, effect, or advantage: *to act to good purpose.*

To <u>set</u> as an aim, intention, or goal for oneself. to intend; design. to resolve to do something. (from dictionary.com)

The etymological base of this old French word carries two understandings. One is "por," which means "to place forth or put forth," which points to positioning, and then "pose," which has to do with presentation. Again, positioning has to do with aim, and pose has to do with goals. So let's dig a little deeper. The first thing that comes to my mind is vision and passion. As a woman who knows her CUP size, you need to be clear on both. How are you going to arrive at your destination if you are not clear on the direction you are going? Let's say you were planning a trip with some girlfriends. The first decision that needs to be made is where you're going, and your vision should be filled with details about your destination or your destiny. Then, after you are clear on where you're going with your vision, your next plan is how, and that's important too, but not as important. It's important because it could make or break the trip, because "a vision without a strategy is a curse," according to Mike Murdock. So, to be clear on our purpose, we must first outline our vision. Then there is the pose, which has to do with passion. Now, before you start a mental ramble, please proceed with caution because your passion is tantamount to your purpose, and one actually points to and leads to the other.

I want also as we discover your purpose for you to understand the dynamics from which purpose is derived. Whenever people ask me how they discover their purpose, I ask them a simple question: "What is your passion?" The reason I ask them this question is simple, because whatever you are passionate about is most likely what your purpose is. I say it unapologetically, because your job is really the place that is supposed to provide you with an income while you are preparing to do your passion. Now please don't get me wrong—the world is full of people who are career minded, career driven, and focused, and there is nothing wrong with working in your field or career path all the way through to retirement. However, if that is not your be-all and end-all, then you need to tap internally and find out what you are passionate about. As the old adage goes, find out what it is here on earth that you love doing so much that if you could, you would do it for free, and then find a way for people to pay you to do it. Case in point, I have a very dear, dear friend who worked as a beautician for years, and what was interesting is although she loved cooking and was very passionate about cooking, she still had a growing child (a boy at that) whom she had to provide for. Well, she was around food all her life, and for as long as she could remember, her grandmother was a cook and had owned a bakery, and her dad was a chef, and she always had this passion about cooking. One day, she started posting pictures on Facebook of the different meals that she had prepared and some of the recipes she created. All of a sudden, people were asking, "How much would you charge to make me a tray of those or a meal for four?" Since then, she has made a decent living at selling plates right out of her kitchen while still being able to support herself financially. My point is that she tapped into her passion and found a way to get people to pay her for her passion, and as a result, she has written several cookbooks and now has a cooking show, and also prepares home-cooked meals for some very famous and popular individuals.

Know the Difference Between the Two *A*'s

There are two *a* words that will also help you discover your purpose. One of them will cause you to prosper, and if you are not careful, the other will cause you to perish.

They are "ambitions" and "assignments." Know the difference between your ambitions and God's assignment. Ambitions are not all bad, but truth be told, it all boils down to motives. Your ambitions will lead you to do things that are mainly self-serving because of your ego and sometimes an envious or a covetous nature and cause you to compromise because you want a certain level of wealth for the wrong reasons. Ambitions have to be weighed in the balances to make sure that they are healthy. I've discovered that when you are blinded by your own ambitions, it will wear you out and drain you physically and mentally. However, when you are on your God-given assignment, things that were once difficult become easy. I don't want to suggest that just because you are walking in your assignment that there won't be opposition and trials. However, when you are in step with the Creator's will, it comes with bonuses. The Bible says in Proverbs 10:22 (KJV), "The blessing of the LORD, it maketh rich, and he addeth no sorrow with it." That word "sorrow" there is translated as "painful toil or labor." Simply put, when He is involved and you are walking in or operating in your assignment, then you won't have to worry or work as hard because things that used to require a lot of your energy become easy because you found your assignment. Your passion is how you gauge this phase of your CUP size because you must understand that your purpose will not come from an outside source. Outside sources may confirm or may inspire because sometimes you do need a model or an example that piques your interest, and when you attempt a thing you are truly passionate about, it will not require much effort because it will come naturally instead of forcefully. It's more to do with choice than chores.

So ask yourself, what is in this world that you would do that you love so much that you would do it for free or all the time if you could? Now I say, please don't limit yourself or think small. Always keep in mind that God's dream for you is always bigger than your dream for yourself. For instance—I have another confession—I can't type, yet I'm not letting that hinder me from authoring this book, and I love writing and didn't even know it until I gave it a try, and now my work will live forever.

Your Purpose Will Lead to Your Wealth

18 "But thou shalt remember the LORD thy God: for *it is* he that giveth thee power to get wealth, that he may establish his covenant which he sware unto thy fathers, as *it is* this day."

Deuteronomy 8:18 (KJV)

The word "power" here is translated as "thought and idea," unlike normally when it is translated as "explosive or authoritative." So if he gives us thought and idea to get wealth, it is up to us to operate in the development of the thought and idea process to bring it out of us and our minds into reality. That's why I always tell people that if God gives you a dream or a thought or you get an idea, write it down and at least check into it. Also, allow me to be clear on the fact that this should be done prayerfully. Why do I say that? Because every good idea is not a God idea. It's a good idea to get married, but it's not a God idea to marry someone you just met with no underwriting. And notice He refers in the aforementioned scripture to the power or thought and idea to get wealth. Wealth always follows your purpose, not the other way around. I must admit I used to be a wealth chaser until I learned the hard way that we are not supposed to chase wealth— it's supposed to chase us.

Let me explain. Matthew 6:33 (KJV) says, "But seek ye first the kingdom of God, and his righteousness; and all these things shall be added unto you."

Matthew admonishes us to seek, go after, and pursue the Kingdom— "king" is short for God, and "dom" is short for "dominion," for way of doing things, so let's read it this way: "Seek ye first God's way of doing things, and watch the result." All these other things which He mentions earlier in the passage, such as clothes, food, and necessities, shall be added unto you. Now pay attention to the word "added." it is a Greek word "pros-tith-ay-mee." It gives the idea of something that comes up behind you or beside you and tackles you down and lies on top of you. When you seek His way of doing things, the stuff you need and desire, you no longer have to chase, but it will chase after you and tackle you down and lie on top of you. When I go after God's way and purpose and assignment for my life, the stuff I chase like cash, cars, clothes, cribs, and creature comforts, come after me, chases me down, and tackles me and lies on top of me. That'll preach, as they say where I'm from in the country.

So let's recap. You now know where to look for your purpose and how to identify it: it's inside of you. That's the location, the manifestation of it, or the way you identify it. It's signified in your passion. Lastly, we discovered that it causes you not to struggle, and it also activates wealth to come after you.

Control Freaks Need Not Apply

You've heard it said that in order to gain control, you must first be willing to lose control. Well, let me manage your expectation by saying that you are never going to be in control 100 percent of the time. You may attempt to control, but the truth of the matter is that you've got to trust that God knows how to handle things a lot better than you do. Let me get the big elephant out of the room by saying that you can't go around with an attitude that says, "If God loved me, why would He allow me to be going through such-and-such?" or "Why would He let so-and-so do me wrong?" Let's be honest. God gave man (meaning us, you, and I) dominion on the earth as free moral agents, and after the fall of man, He allowed Satan to be the prince of the air, which is cool, and considering that all things are working for our good, it simply means that Satan—although he may think he is on cloud nine—is really on our payroll and doesn't know it. Then you have to take under consideration that there is more at work than just God. To say that God is in charge of everything would be like saying He's the cause of rape, murder, molestation, and all the other sinister acts of this world. There's more at work than just God. There are the enemies, people's motives at work, personal agendas at work, wicked politics at work, people's love of money at work, and so on. When you put it all together, you get an understanding that God is not playing puppets with us. You see the bigger picture that we have more power than we think, but unfortunately, some people choose to use their power for sinister reasons.

Attention: your life does not get better by chance; it gets better by change, so if you are going to walk in purpose, there will be some changes; now it will take some patience.

Wait on the Lord

> "*Wait on the LORD, and keep his way, and he shall exalt thee to inherit the land: when the wicked are cut off, thou shalt see it.*"[1]

There are two words this generation abhors, and they are "wait" and "patience." They are not as popular as they are potent. If you have ever gone to a hospital, one of the most stressful places is the waiting room.

[1] Ps. 37:34.

What a mix of emotions and anxiety. It's mainly where families camp out with anticipation that there has been a change in the situations of their loved ones.

Our society has mastered technology, gone to the moon, broken the sound barrier, and now there is talk of trips and tours of outer space, but we can't seem to wait. We've made stairs move and called it an escalator. We took the sperm of a man and the egg of a woman, put it in a test tube, and came up with a little girl and named her Louise. Man is so smart that he was able to come up with a flying bird by hanging tons of steel in the air, which made it possible for you to have breakfast in New York, lunch in Paris, and dinner in Spain. Man is smart. Man is so smart that he took the heart of a monkey, put it in the chest of a man, and made it beat for two months. Man is smart. Man mastered the ionosphere and put a satellite in space that he can control a missile here on earth to destroy his enemies with the push of one button, but man can't seem to wait. Those who are single can't wait to get married. Those who are married can't wait to be single. Those who are young can't wait to be grown, and those of us who are grown wish we could be young. Those who are sick can't wait to get well. Those who are pursuing higher levels of academia can't wait to graduate. But man can't master waiting. From the boardroom to the classroom, from the skidrow to the White House, we struggle with this age-old perplexity: let's get in a hurry to wait.

It's interesting to me that no one has time to do it right, but everyone has time to do it over. I can't blame us for not waiting; it's hereditary. Not waiting has worked in our favor at some points in history. What if those who felt they were held hostage under the religious regime of the king had waited not to seek out discovering America to have independence to worship their God in spirit and in truth? What if Abraham Lincoln had not freed the slaves despite resistance from his own political party? What if Dr. King had not led the march in Washington? What if Rosa Parks had given up her seat? They didn't wait, so what's the difference? They weren't waiting on an opportunity; they trusted the time was right to act, and thus they did it with well-executed plans; because lack of organization only leads to frustration. We're instructed to wait on the Lord. So, David, why would you tell me to wait on the Lord? Here's the answer: so that I may follow *His tracks* so that I may inherit *His treasures* so that I may learn how to trust *His timing*.

He tells me to wait on the Lord and keep His way, however, this is our dilemma. We think we know what is best for us, so we care more about our way than His way. After all, His way takes so long. His way requires me to stretch my patience and retreat when I want to fight. His way requires me to love those who are seemingly unlovable, and oh, that be-nice-to-my-enemies part? I really hate that! But it's all a part of keeping His way. When I think about it, His way is best. "Father knows best" describes His wisdom, overshadowing my whining. For we see in part, we look up to the corner, but He made the corner. We see the problem, but He's already seen the solution. We see the cancer, but He has the cure. He has the answer for my agony, the balm for my bruises. He has the comfort for my crisis. He has deliverance for my dilemmas. The more I think about it, I'd rather do it His way. Elvis did it his own way, and he died. Yeah, when I think about it, I'd better stick with His way. He's already given us the blue-print in His Word, but what's interesting to me is that people who say they love God don't love Him enough to read the only book He ever wrote.

No Need to Reinvent Wheels

I recall hearing a story of a father and son who were caught in a snow storm. They needed wood for the fireplace. The snow was so thick that it came up to the kneecaps of the father. It was so deep that it would have drowned the little boy. So the father told the little boy, "Stand here in the doorway while I go to the woodshed to gather wood for the fire." The father made his trek to the woodshed slowly but surely, step by step through the blizzard-like conditions until he finally arrived. While gathering wood, he heard a noise as though someone was behind him. Startled, he turned around only to discover the young lad standing there, shivering in the cold. His father said, "Son, I told you, it's dangerous out here, and I gave you specific instructions to stay in the house. I want to know why you would come out here, and how did you make it?"

The young boy explained, "Daddy, I came because I was scared, but the way I made it was that everywhere you stepped, I stepped. It was hard, but the tracks you left made it a whole lot easier." That's the same way it is with the Lord. I'm following Him. Sometimes it may get sketchy, but don't get scared when young men get shot down in the street like dogs. I get concerned when I hear of a flip-flop in the stock market like a yo-yo going up and down that threatens the stability of the nation's economy. I don't get scared when I turn on the news to find out that the wrong rates are going up and the right rates are going down; murder rate up, unemployment rate up, graduation rate down. That's scary, but what makes it easier is when I step where He steps. David says to keep His way. You've tried it other ways, but they never seem to work. You might as well try His way.

I also need to keep his way for exaltation, for He promised if I stay in his way, His word, and His will that, He will exalt me. It's almost like David is saying that you get a promise and a promotion. When you stick with the Lord, He gives you double for your trouble. I learned this lesson while serving my pastor. I used to come under attack and ridicule because I attached myself to my pastor. I didn't do it for recognition or reward and I didn't do it because he required it. I did it because it was my reasonable service. People would call me his flunky, among other names that I cannot put in print, but I always noticed something, and that was when I stayed close to my pastor as God elevated him, I was able to get on the elevator because I was with my pastor. When he would go up, I would go up because I was with him. When he got to eat at nice restaurants, I enjoyed the benefits of eating at the same places. That's elevation.

The next clause speaks about the promise, because promotion is an earthly concept, but inheritance has to do with being in the will. People normally get an inheritance after they've waited and someone else has transitioned from earth to glory. If I wait on the Lord, it strategically places me as an heir and a joint heir.

A story is told of a young man whose father loved him very much. He was an only child, and his father was very wealthy. The man was so wealthy that he owned every manner of creature comfort that one could fathom, to say the least. One day, however, the young man got drafted in a war. Not long thereafter, he was killed. Upon hearing the news, the father was distraught and overtaken with depression. He had a picture of his son painted and hung over the fireplace as a memorial. He loved that boy. There was an old man who worked for the father and had witnessed the father sitting around the fireplace every day, looking at the picture of his beloved son.

One day, the father died, and there was an auction to auction off the father's earthly belongings. People came from miles around in hopes of bidding on these earthly treasures. The auctioneer arrived that day, set up his makeshift podium, and stated that the first item up for bid was the picture of the man's son.

"What do I hear? Do I hear five dollars?" No one said a word. "Do I hear ten dollars?" No one said a word. The gentleman who worked for the father was present that day and knew how the father felt about the son, so he raised his hand and bid on the picture. The auctioneer said, "Going once, going twice, sold to the man in the rear." The auctioneer commenced closing up his case, packing up his podium, and walked toward the door.

The crowd was enraged, inciting a possible riot. When asked, "What are you doing, Mr. auctioneer? Don't you see all the expensive paintings, custom cars, furs and such left to auction? We are here to bid on them."

The auctioneer, after calming the crowd, said these words: "My apologies, but the man left in his will that whoever takes his son can have everything else he owned." Well, those of us who wait, we are in his will, and because we accepted his son, we have access to everything our Father in Heaven owns.

Lastly, waiting on the Lord helps me to accept His timing. My time is in His hands. Our problem with time is that we live in time, but we serve a God who's not bound by any time. His birthday is before "in the beginning," and last I checked, there is no death date on record. There's one process David says that cannot be avoided or averted and that is the process of time. You must understand that God runs a risk when He blesses us because if we get it out of season, and before time, it will mess us up, or we will mess it up. You don't give a Bentley or a Rolls-Royce to a twelve-year-old—it's not time yet. You don't marry two fourteen-year-olds—that's not the time for that. You don't start a business right after giving birth to a baby. You don't promote a new employee on his or her first day on the job. You don't take a novice and place him or her over seasoned saints. Why, you ask? It's not the time. Someone has said that it is never the right time if you are waiting for it. This can be confused with procrastination, but I contend that there is one time that is right, and that is the Lord's time. Why His time? Because He wants to display you as a trophy so that even your enemies can see you shine. It may get dark, but wait. You may have some fiery furnaces, and you may get thrown into some pits and thrown into jail for a crime you didn't commit. You might have to go through some lions' dens; and lastly, they may nail you to a cross on a Friday but just wait—Sunday morning is coming. I love you to life, not to death. Wait, I say, on the Lord.

It's Your Thang—Do What You Wanna Do!

I would be remiss if I didn't throw in this little helpful hint to tell you not to forget that He gave us all a thought or a thing that we do well, so no matter how insignificant you may think it is, use it. It may be tweaking something you have, but make the adjustment. You have proof around you; we don't have to even look in the Bible to see people who used what they have. Let me introduce you to a woman who found her purpose in the strangest place. She is an American businesswoman and founder of a multimillion-dollar company.

She is the world's youngest self-made female billionaire. In 2012, she was named in the "Time 100," an annual list of the one hundred most influential people in the world assembled by *Time*. She was born on February 21, 1971 in Clearwater, Florida the daughter of a trial attorney and an artist. She attended Clearwater High School and graduated from Florida State University with a degree in communications. She was a member of Delta Delta Delta sorority. Her plan to become an attorney was altered after twice doing poorly on the LSAT, and she instead took a job at Walt Disney World in Orlando, Florida where she worked for three months. She also worked as a stand-up comedian from time to time.

After her short stint at Disney, she accepted a job with Danka, an office supply company where she sold fax machines door-to-door. She was quite successful in sales and was promoted to national sales trainer at the age of twenty-five. Having been forced to wear pantyhose in the hot Florida climate, she disliked the appearance of the seamed foot while wearing open-toed shoes but liked the fact that the control-top eliminated panty lines and made the body appear firmer. She experimented by cutting off the feet of her pantyhose while wearing them under a new pair of slacks; unfortunately the experiment was not successful, as the pantyhose continuously rolled up her leg.

At age twenty-seven, she moved to Atlanta, and while still working at Danka, spent the next two years and $5,000 she had set aside in her savings researching hosiery patents and visiting craft stores to find the right material for her product. Eventually coming upon a solution, she wrote her own patent from a Barnes & Noble textbook and incorporated her company. Turned away by numerous mills that did not see the value of her idea, she eventually found a hosiery factory in Asheboro, North Carolina that was willing to make her product. She successfully pitched her idea to Neiman-Marcus by personally taking the buyer to the ladies' restroom to show her the benefits of the invention in person. Bloomingdales, Saks, and Bergdorf Goodman soon followed. She handled all aspects of the business from marketing, logistics, and product positioning (preferring that her product be sold alongside shoes rather than in hosiery). In November 2000, Oprah Winfrey named her product her favorite product of the year and sales took off. Soon after, she resigned from Danka. Her company had $4 million in sales in its first year and $10 million in sales in its second year. In 2001, she signed a contract with QVC, the home shopping channel, where she sold eight thousand pairs of her product in the first six minutes. Her name is Sara Blakely and her product is SPANX!

History reveals that the creator gave us all a purpose, and what you do best or are passionate about and love more than anything could be your purpose. Maybe it's solving a problem for women like Sara Blakely, but whatever it is, use what's in your hand. It's your thang.

He gave Adam a rib, Noah an axe, Moses a rod, Dorcas a needle, Sampson strength, David a slingshot, Famous Amos a cookie recipe, Colonel Sanders eleven herbs and spices, Michael Jordan a basketball, Dr. Martin Luther King Jr. a dream, Maya Angelou a poem, and Tyler Perry the character Madea. I ask you today, what's in your hand?

Partnering Is a Part of the Plan

The final thing I want to say about purpose is that there are some tools involved. You were never meant to go it alone. Sometimes you are going to have to come off the island of sheroism for a moment and understand the power of partnerships. You are going to need some help. There are three things you must remember. First, you have got to pick your posse wisely. This means get away from people who have your problem and get around people who have your answer. People who have your problem are always pulling you or holding you down because misery really does love company. Second, you are too old for games, so simplify. You need people who can compliment you and not complicate you. By all means get this in your spirit. Don't allow people to bring you their "strama"—that's stress and drama mixed together. Third, remain humble. Don't get the big head. What it took you twenty years to build up God can take twenty seconds and tear it all down. Courage is only rage under control.

Partnerships are imperative to progress. Just like the concentric lines of a bull's eye are necessary to one another to make the target, so should we align with partnerships to make life goals more reachable and rewarding. You see, my sister, relationships are not all about finding your significant other to fall in love and run off and live happily ever after with. "Relationship" simply means there is something you need that I have and something that I need that you have, but if we never partner, we will never discover what those purposes and possibilities are; therefore, it would behoove us to be partners. We are all someone's answer. You are actually only as valuable as your willingness to solve the problems of those around you. Now don't get me wrong, I'm not saying for you to put on a Wonder Woman suit and go around rescuing everyone. What I am saying is that just as you are someone's answer or hold someone's answer, someone likewise may hold your answer.

Partnerships have been behind some of the biggest Fortune 500 and Fortune 100 companies for ages. Consider Henry Sherwin and Edward Williams back in 1866. One was a banker and the other a paint developer who liked experimenting around with different colors and thought that existing paints were so limiting and dull. They figured out how to partner and set out to paint the world, which has been their company's motto for well over a hundred years now, and they are one of the premier companies—if not *the* premier paint company in the world worth upward of $7.6 billion. You know them as the Sherwin-Williams Company.

In addition there other examples of partnerships like Rolls-Royce. The history of Rolls-Royce dates back to 1904 when Henry Royce was introduced to Charles Rolls in Manchester. Royce had run an electrical and mechanical business since 1884 while Rolls was one of Britain's first car dealers. The thing that brought the two men together however, was the two-cylinder Royce 10 that was made by Royce in 1904. Rolls preferred three and four-cylinder cars; however, he was so impressed by Royce's two-cylinder vehicle that he promised him to take as many Royce's cars as he could make. Royce and Rolls reached an agreement according to which four models would be made, all would bear Rolls-Royce name, and they would be sold exclusively by Rolls. The first Rolls-Royce two-cylinder car was presented at the Paris Salon at the end of 1904.

In 1906, the two entrepreneurs partnered and formed Rolls-Royce Limited and started to look for an appropriate location for a car production factory. They considered several locations, including Manchester where Royce had a factory, but they eventually decided on Derby because the city council offered them cheap electricity. The Rolls-Royce factory in Derby was designed by Royce and the production began in 1908.

As they say, the rest is history.

I could go on with examples spanning from Exxon Mobil to how truck stops such as Love's are partnering with restaurants like Wendy's to make the road-trip vacation experience more memorable; yet if you don't get it into your spirit, you may be denying yourself wealth and opportunity, so don't try to do it all by yourself. If you don't check yourself, you may not only wreck yourself, but you may, baby girl, find yourself all by yourself.

Again, my friend, find your passion and it will lead you to your purpose—and don't rule out partnership.

CHAPTER 7

What Does He Keep Staring At?
The Real Reason Why Men Look!

Okay, let's be honest. You've sometimes wondered why men stare. Why is it that sometimes men just seem to lose their bearings around women? They can't focus on what you're saying because they are glued and zeroed in on what you are wearing. And then there is the side of you that wants him to pay more attention to what's in you not what's on you. After all, forget baby got back; you want him to know baby got brains, but when he sees you, he just keeps staring.

So, you want the truth, but can you handle the truth? I hate to be the bearer of bad news, but, ladies, there is a vast difference in the way that men have been wired. Men are visual. Normally, men will make decisions that are based on what they see, whereas women make decisions from the seats of their emotions. You see, great woman that you are, men are goal oriented—that's why they always, for the most part, are looking for something or someone to conquer or boss, even if it's nothing but a dog. Men like knowing that they have achieved some sort of reward, thus explaining why men compete in everything from sports to checkers. Not that this is a good thing, but men originally, from our earliest existence were hunters. Pursuit was what gave us the adrenaline to conquer and devour, and then we were on to the next challenge. It's in the genes and the nature. That's why men get bored in relationships so quickly. After they feel that they have conquered (won) you, they start looking for the next challenge. Don't take it personally.

On the other hand, women, unlike men, aren't always as goal oriented as they are security oriented. A woman wants to know that she has some security because when you arrived on the scene, everything you needed was already in place. A real woman wants to know that the bills are paid and that regardless to who brought home the bacon, it's in the freezer or refrigerator. Plus, women want to be assured and affirmed. That's why a woman will sit in a beauty shop for four hours—she wants you to tell her that she looks good.

Unless they invent a pill that will shut it off, ladies, *we stare*. Sorry on behalf of the male race, but that's the way we are wired. Now help us out a little. Not all men will undress you with their eyes. Sometimes a man is just in awe and admiration of the beautiful vessel of a specimen you are. A man is normally thinking that you are willing to share what you are willing to show. So that doesn't mean that you walk around looking like a freshly erased chalkboard. It means that it's okay to be presentable without being provocative. Just be able to handle the stares or the references to being eye candy. But can we be honest, ladies? You may complain that men look, but sometimes y'all dress a certain way on purpose because you are what my bestie calls an "attention whore." Excuse the language but those are the women who love to be the center of attention. They're not going to bust a grape at a fruit fight or throw rice at a wedding, but they dress to get the attention, and so we stare.

So You Want to Shift His Focus

Now, this is the problem. I must speak to three different women on this subject. First is the single woman who is trying to attract the man she wants. Then there's the married woman who wants the man she has to want her back. And thirdly, there's the woman who is content with herself and where she is in being single.

So let's break the code.

First, there's the single woman. As much as you hate to accept it, you gals outnumber us, and in these days, it's competitive. Now don't get mad at me for this, but hey, let's be honest; yes, I know you were taught to be hidden and let him find you and all the cute Christian clichés; however, let's look at a passage that you may not have been taught in Sunday school.

> 1 And in that day seven women shall take hold of one man, saying, We will eat our own bread, and wear our own apparel: only let us be called by thy name, to take away our reproach.
>
> Isaiah 4:1 (KJV)
>
> 1 AND IN that day seven women shall take hold of one man, saying, We will eat our own bread and provide our own apparel; only let us be called by your name to take away our reproach [of being unmarried].
>
> Isaiah 4:1–2 (AMP)

¹ In that day seven women will take hold of one man and say, "We will eat our own food and provide our own clothes; only let us be called by your name. Take away our disgrace!"

Isaiah 4:1–2 (NIV)

¹ At that time so few men will be left alive that seven women will fight over each of them and say, "Let us all marry you! We will furnish our own food and clothing; only let us be called by your name so that we won't be mocked as old maids."

Isaiah 4:1 (TLB)

¹ That will be the day when seven women will gang up on one man, saying, "We'll take care of ourselves, get our own food and clothes. Just give us a child. Make us pregnant so we'll have something to live for!"

Isaiah 4:1 (MSG)

I printed this in five different versions so that you will not get angry at me or think I'm going back on what I said earlier. I tend to be an old-fashioned guy. However, I have to take in account that everyone doesn't think like I do. And if you are honest, everyone doesn't think like you, either, so let's look at what this text implies.

First, it speaks about what is going on in society right at this moment. Let's look at the math (seven women to every man), the mess (the fighting), the misleading (the independence and freeing him of responsibility), the mistake (marriage is not about being desperate, it's about being in destiny), and the mirage (what people are thinking because we hate looking bad).

First, the math. Well, the sad reality is that we have a numbers imbalance. Statistics show that we are in the seven to 1 ratio; however, because babies are being born every day and with the prison population of males increasing daily—and I'm not going to even mention the HIV crisis—therefore if you continue to add the numbers, no one really knows. Allow me to narrow it even further and say that when you consider eligible men, that changes the numbers yet again; so it's safe to assume that there are probably seven women to every man. But, I beg of you, don't let this deter you, because knowing your CUP size will help you see this not as the market being competitive but as this being your opportunity to prove that you are not thirsty, desperate, needy, or greedy because you have a standard, and the numbers don't make you lose focus. You are the prize at the end of the day because six more women have to measure up to who you are, so the six have mighty big shoes to fill because now you know your calling, your uniqueness, and your purpose. So you, my dear, are a step ahead of the game.

Let's look at the mess the passage shares. The mess is that it says these seven women will take hold, gang up on, and then (as two versions say) fight over a man. That's a hot, trifling mess. Well, we know this passage is not describing women who know their CUP sizes because you, girlfriend, are neither desperate nor are you fighting over *any* man. If there's going to be some fighting, it had better be over you. I get so disheartened nowadays when I see these what I refer to as not-our-reality shows like *Mob Wives*, *Housewives of* this city or that city; *Love & Hip Hop*, and others showing women belittling and berating themselves by fighting over a man. To me, it is so degrading to see women fighting over men. Sometimes they are not even men they are married to. This is a psychological conundrum that needs to be dealt with because if there is any question as to you being the one-and-only woman in his life or if there is another woman in the picture, that's a fidelity issue that doesn't need a fight—it needs clarity of relationship boundaries; yet, in this context, it's referring to a shortage of male inventory. This yields another problem—men shouldn't be viewed as inventory like TVs or iPads at Christmas where people stand in lines forever and trample one another and fight for the last like there won't be any more available. So let's abase and place this mess in perspective;

Never, under any circumstances, should you allow another woman to pull you into a fight over a man. And let's just say he is your husband—it's not about defending your honor at that point; it's about choices. Did he choose her over you, or is he choosing to reconcile and never see her again? And if he chooses her, then your fight should be spiritual warfare, not physical altercations. Then there is the sad reality that maybe that season is over because one person's loss is another's gain, but never lower yourself to the point of desperate measures that you devalue another woman or yourself and put yourself in harm's way. Plainly put, hands are for helping, not for hurting. Now I hear you saying that I'm not a woman and that I don't understand your pain. Well, that's like saying I need to smoke crack to tell people not to do it because it kills. I say this to you from the premise of empowering yourself, not to minimize your hurt. What I am saying is— get hold of your emotions. The Bible says that we are supposed to bring our emotions and feelings under subjection. I've had plenty of broken hearts and disappointments. Like Gladys Knight said, I've had my share of life's ups and downs, so I just want you to be clear that feelings should never escalate to fights, because anger is one letter short of danger. He's not worth it; the other woman's not worth it, but you are.

Ladies, please note the following statements are not to suggest that men should be compared to dogs:

There should be no fighting for three reasons. First, always remember that a well-fed dog won't run away from home. We used to have a dog a German shepherd named Duke. I loved Duke. He was my childhood best friend, and we kept Duke fed. He ate like we ate, and my momma cooked like she was cooking for an army, but even if he got off his chain, or as we say, "got loose," he would never go farther than our house and a care home that my mother had up the street, two doors down from our house, and he would guard both houses. But he knew where home was. My point is simple—if he leaves, don't internalize it as you weren't doing your part, it may be that he's greedy and doesn't realize what he has at home. Second, there should be no physical fighting because you insult God. You may be wondering, how? Well, we are made in God's image, and He dwells in us even when we don't act like His children. We are representatives of God so if you wouldn't hit or strike God, then you should have the same respect for those created in His image. Third and finally, you are just better than that. Always remember whatever God runs out of, He can always make more of it, so the fact that there would even seemingly be a man-shortage is ludicrous because God has some eligible males waiting to find their queens, and also don't count out the one you deemed no good. God is still a miracle worker. Just look at you.

Moreover there is the misleading. The text says they will say we will buy our own food and clothes. Basically, we will take care of ourselves. What an admirable trait it is to be independent. Yeah, the old "You don't need a man" clarion call. But the truth is that you may feel like you don't *need* a man, yet at some point there will be a part of your womanhood that desires a man. These women Isaiah is describing are so blinded by wanting to fit in that they compromise God's plan and play *Let's Make a Deal* with destiny. Allow me to say there is nothing wrong with having your own and doing for yourself and having your own money and being a self-made woman, but don't send the wrong message and mess up his opportunity to prove that he can be the head and take up the slack. Don't be a gold digger, but don't be a damsel in distress, either. This is a balancing act, because when Mr. Right comes along and he sees you've got your own castle and you are the queen bee in charge, it could be interpreted two or more ways. A man could see that and say, "Well, she's the queen, and she's got it covered, so there's no place for me to come along and be the king." Or it could be interpreted for the opportunist as what they call in the hood a "come up," and he looks for a way to capitalize on your labor. That's a snake stay away from him. Remember, "Every man walks in the directions of applause." Men want to feel that there is a need for their input and strength, but here is the secret: every real man is looking for a woman that is doing her so well, that he sees an opportunity to add value and covering to her. Don't be needy; just make him feel needed.

Another issue is the mistake. One version says, "Just let us have your name." Another version suggests that they say "Give us a child." There's that desperate spirit again. First, let me say that it looks like these women in Isaiah were busy trying to hook a man rather than hiding so that they might be found. The Bible says, "He that findeth a wife." But you can't find what's not hiding. You can't unwrap a gift that has no paper on it. The danger in this thinking pattern is that people fail to realize that normally what it takes to get a person is what it takes to keep that person, so don't be in a hurry to get someone down the aisle. Remember, marriage is not about the wedding, it's about God's will. It's not about the diamond, it's about destiny. You don't get married just because it seems like you both have something in common. Don't be so in a hurry that you marry a stranger and choose carats over character—or that you want his name but don't trust his nature. You shouldn't get married because you are sexually frustrated. You get married because your destiny is tied to your partner's destiny; not because your biological clock is ticking. Marriage takes work—and lots of it, so please don't mess anyone's life up on a wish and a whim.

Finally there is the mirage. This is how the writer and penman so delicately put it—"So we won't be disgraced," one says. "So we won't be looked at as old maids in the city." In other words, image and reputation were more important than joy, peace, and love. They seemed preoccupied by—or rather slaves of—poor self-image and other people's opinions. Please do us both a favor and get free of other people's opinions. Don't compromise comfort for cuteness and don't risk it all for image, because the same people who brought gifts to the wedding will tweet about you on Twitter or post your divorce announcement on Facebook. Stop worrying yourself over people's opinions, and concentrate on being prepared to be the mate God called you to be, and if you are married, become more of a cheerleader and not a critic. Remember, every man walks in the direction of applause.

Men are going to look because we are visual. Don't get offended, get over it. He may not be staring because he's a pervert; He may feel you are perfect. Sometimes we admire what we desire.

CHAPTER 8

Your Headlights Are On:
Following Your Intuition and Getting a Grip on Life

I'll never forget the time when I was out on a date. Yes, pastors can go out on dates. Don't get your undies in a bunch. I was out on a date at a restaurant here in Columbus called Roosters. I love going there because they have these little placards up all over the place that are like little epigraphs, and I love humor and reading. One of them said, "I used to have a handle on life, but it broke." This saying provoked me to think about how many more people have settled with going through life when it seemingly had gotten away from them, and so I wanted to say that something in your own life lesson may have broken or has seemingly gotten away from your grasp, but guess what? You can get a grip on life again, because now that you know your CUP size, nothing else has to slip from your grip.

It was 2005—in September, to be more exact, and yes, it was a great year. I had dabbled in real estate before and bought some rental properties. This was the year I purchased my first home. I've always been forward thinking, and I have to attribute a lot of that to my father. So when I originally purchased the home, it was just me so I really didn't want to live there alone because that was way too much space for me, bxzut I figured that I would eventually get married and that I would have a nice home to move my wife into and my family if she had children or if I chose to start a family of my own. Also, I was purchasing the house because it was an investment. Remember, my parents taught me and reared me to be a provider. The house had five bedrooms, four and a half bathrooms, a five-car garage, an in-law suite, two fireplaces, and One day, because I traveled so much as an itinerant preacher/speaker, I decided to just enjoy my beautiful home. I disrobed and retired downstairs to the lower level to sit in the dry-heat sauna. I was utterly caught off guard and surprised as I opened the door to the sauna and turned on the light, and there was a spiderweb the size of China. Okay, maybe I'm exaggerating, but it was huge. Out of sheer panic, I rushed upstairs, found the yellow pages, and commenced to calling an exterminator. I wanted the problem fixed the day before yesterday.

The exterminator sent a gentleman out the next day. After assessing the web, I knew he was going to call in the crew, and they put an APB (all points bulletin) on this spider. What he said to me changed my viewpoint, although it was not the answer I was looking for, especially coupled with the fact that I was terrified of spiders. In high school, a young lady I dated was bitten by a brown recluse spider and almost died from the bite. So I justifiably had reason to panic.

Anyway, he said to me, "You don't want to get rid of that spider."

I was like, "Excuse me, sir, but anything that resides in my house has to have a job and help pay some bills."

He said, "No, you don't understand. That particular spider eats up poisonous and unwanted insects and creepy-crawling things." So in other words, the spider was a good one.

I said to him, "Well, how can you tell?"

He said, "Just look at the beauty of the web."

It was that day that I learned a lesson about spiders and getting a grip.

Lessons from the Strangest Things

The spider taketh hold with her hands, and is in kings' palaces.

—Proverbs 30:28

Little Miss Muffet sat on a tuffet, eating her curds whey. Along came a spider, which sat down beside her, and frightened Miss Muffet away. The words of that nursery rhyme many of us heard, recited, and then committed to memory as children. It struck a fear in us that spiders must mean or translate as "bad." Now, don't get me wrong, there are some species of spiders you don't want to be in proximity of. However, there are some life lessons that we can learn just by noticing the nature of the spider. First, get over the psychological imprisonment of mental pictures, and pay attention. Pay attention to what, you might ask. Pay attention to the obvious. Have you ever noticed that humans kill more spiders than spiders kill humans? I mean, here I was at that time, nearly three hundred pounds of big, strong, muscular man, and I was afraid of something that didn't weigh three ounces. If anything, the spider should have been afraid of me. I felt so stupid when I thought about it. I bring up this fact because, as a woman who now knows her CUP size, you have to do away with foolish fears and things that you have built a case against in your mind. You must begin to deal with issues you used to run from, no matter how large or small. It may be your fear of heights or flying or other things that used to prevent you from living in the fullness of life. Yes, you are going to have to build a bridge and get over it. It may be something as small as having a critical and crucial conversation with someone you have been avoiding to deal with a sensitive subject matter that has you stuck in a bad place or frozen in a bad experience from your childhood, and now you find yourself thirty-years-old dealing with a thirteen-year-old girl's problems. Yes, I am in Bible country because God has not given us the spirit of fear but of power, love, and a sound mind.

I acknowledge the fact that many of us don't like spiders, and oftentimes we get a leery and frightening feeling at the mention of spiders, but beyond that, look at the text. It says that "the spider taketh hold with her hands." It almost seems like a mistake because we all know spiders don't have hands like we do, but their feet are like our hands. They use them to get a grip on things. Have you ever felt like life was slipping away from you? Well, here are four things about spiders that are interesting and will help us "get a grip."

First, let's look at the *work* of the spider. Yes, I was shocked, but spiders have a job, a purpose, and a place, just like you and I. Notice that she "taketh hold with her hands," which shows her initiative and her intention. She didn't wait for stuff to happen. She took the initiative to make things happen. I want you to put this in your pipe and smoke it. Get out of the apathetic mind-set that you are so special and different that life ought to fall in your lap. Some stuff is not going to happen to you until you first learn how to happen to it. You've got to take hold of some stuff. I know you may not be a football fan, but in sports terms, you've got to tackle it. Learn to be assertive—a go-getter. I tell you, the graveyard is full of people who were waiting on their ships to come in. Now don't get me wrong, I know that in a previous chapter I mentioned waiting on the Lord. That had to do with divine direction, however, this assertiveness I am speaking of is using what you have to get where you are going—not standing on the sideline being critical of others who are in the game and on the field, but participation and not just observation. Janet Jackson used to have a song that said, "What have you done for me lately?" Well, from a male perspective, we want to know, what have *you* done for you lately? I cannot stress it enough that most men want to see you doing so well that they have to try to figure out how to enhance and improve on the foundation. "The spider taketh hold with her hands"—that's work. She knows intuitively that she has a web to spin and that it won't get spun on its own, so she taketh hold. She gets a grip on her location. She plans out in her mind where she's going to start. I've seen women who were models, and to see them walk the runway was amazing. Some of them looked as if they were floating on air. But backstage was a whole crew of makeup artists and seamstresses who were working to make them look that good. It takes some work. You don't get a six-pack sitting on the couch watching the *Maury* show; you have to get in the gym and work. You don't become a real estate mogul watching infomercials, hoping they are mailing you the latest and greatest gadget. You've got to go out and ride neighborhoods looking for the deals. Somebody yell, "Work it!"

But the spider did it intentionally of her own will and volition. In life, take cues from the spider. Don't wait for things to happen; make things happen with your hands. Like the scripture says, "whatsoever your hands find to do, do it."

Next, there is the *wealth* of the spider, which is her web. In other words, her wealth came from within her and not from outside of her. Could it be that you are looking for your wealth in all the wrong places? What you seek may not be on the outside; it's possibly on the inside. Yes, I have come to serve notice, my sister—no matter what color, what creed, what race, or what your background is, your wealth is an inside job. They have a reality show that used to come on called *Hoarders*, and it was showing people who had seemingly checked out of life, and very likely, there were some mental health issues. I remember so well watching an episode where this one woman had just given up on life after the death of her husband. It was amazing because she not only quit life, but she pushed away anybody and everybody who cared anything about her, like her kids, and no one could seem to reach her. The house was loaded from floor to ceiling in every room with nothing but trash and debris and even fecal matter and rodents. It was a safety-hazard nightmare. She had collected so much junk and stuff over the years and would never throw anything away. They finally convinced her to allow them to come in and help clear out the house to make it inhabitable again, and they began to throw out things that seemingly were of no value, and it was thought when they began that she was just a poor old lady, but as they begin to sort through her things, they found valuable paintings, rare coins, and jewelry that had been passed down from her great-great-grandparents, which were worth hundreds of thousands, if not millions, of dollars. But, there was one problem—It was in the house buried under all of her junk.

Girlfriend, maybe it's time for you to declutter your life and sort through the junk piles of debris from yesteryear. You may have so many hidden treasures in the house—or better yet, inside of you. Maybe it's time to take those music lessons or that dance class or that art class or to go on that expedition. You have so many untapped gifts and talents that it's unbelievable.

The spider's wealth comes from inside of her. When a spider spins a web, she does it with design and with detail. In other words, she does it on purpose and with precision, not just a line here and a line there. Webs are designed that way because she has a pattern. The word "excellence" means that you pay attention to the details. Your wealth is an inside job. That dream and desire God placed in you is unique and is there for a reason. If he put it in you, it's your job to bring it out of you.

Then there's the *wisdom* of the spider. This wisdom is twofold. She knows how to walk on her web. Have you ever noticed how a spider can walk all over a web, and if you touch the web with a broom or your hand, its sticks to you? Well, that's because a spider has oil in her feet that allows her to walk on the web with no problem. Without trying to sound "too deep" (as we say in the church world), oil is a sign of anointing; so she's been anointed to walk on the web. That is why I want you to know and embrace the uniqueness of your CUP size. Like the spider walks all over her web, you've been anointed to walk on your web. That's why I hate the fallacy that people often have about blessings as if they are some sort of football that you have to clench and run for the goal line in fear of it being stripped. No, that's not how it works. Your blessing was anointed for you, and you were anointed for it, so much so that if I got what was yours, I couldn't do anything with it.

Not only was she designed and given the wisdom to walk on her web, there is also the wisdom of discernment. If you look closely enough, the spider can discern and sense when someone is near the web or if the web is being disturbed. It's as if the spider senses when danger is near. Well, you have that same discernment if you pay attention to your spirit. Now, if you are a person who is suspect of everything and everybody, then you are not going to get it. I am speaking of being tapped in and tuned in to the intuition that God has given us called the spirit of discernment. You remember how the older folks used to say, "I got a feeling about so-and-so"? Or they would say that something was telling them that maybe you shouldn't go out to the club, and then later you discover that someone got hurt or shot or some tragedy befell them. That was not just mother's wit; that was the Holy Spirit nudging them and inspiring them to warn you and me that something wasn't right. My point is that you'd better get a grip on your discerning wisdom, because that may save you a lot of heartache and heartbreak.

Remember, you are anointed to walk on your web. There is an oil on your feet that other people don't have for your particular web or assignment. If I got your blessing, I couldn't do anything with it because I haven't been anointed to handle it, but you have. Lastly on this point, I would like to point out the design of the spider's wisdom. They spin their webs by design. Looking back on my experience of finding that gigantic web—it really was a work of beauty. It wasn't a line here and a line there—it was a work of art. Everything was connected and orderly. My sister, you have to have some wisdom to do some things by design. Don't just do a bunch of stuff and then go close your eyes and cross your fingers and pray and hope it works out. Have a design, a pattern, a plan, and connect the dots. Be vigilant, be viable, be veracious. The spider does it by design. The word "wisdom" is a compound word—"wis" is short for "wise," and "dom" is short for "dominion," which means "way of doing things." There is a wise way of doing things.

Now, if there is a wise way of doing things, there is also a foolish way. Be wise. Being wise means doing things on purpose and in purpose, like having a savings nest egg put away in case the company closes down so that you won't go into total shock. Being wise means not always living trying to impress folks. Live out your God-given vision—not what your family expects or what your friends think is best, but what gives you joy. Have a design for your health and wealth; and your leisure and your life.

Then lastly, there is the *will* of the spider. I must say I saved this one for last. I'm so impressed with the spider's will. Have you ever noticed that when you knock down a spider's web, she normally goes right back to where the last one got destroyed, and she picks up where she left off? That's good news because somebody may have destroyed your web, but I come to declare and decree unto you that you can pick up where you left off. So what if you dropped out of school? There is still night school. So what if you had a baby out of wedlock? Life still goes on. So what if your first business failed? Just pick up where you left off, reevaluate, pray, and sense the leading of God because He will give you the go-ahead and you will end up like the spider in kings' palaces. Get a grip. Yes, that thing that's inside of you will land you in palaces and places that you never dreamed of.

At the time of this writing, I am on a mission trip in the island of Saint Kitts in the West Indies. The year 2013 was one of rebellion. I was rejected by my former church and was left with nothing. But, I heard an old country singer say that there's nothing wrong with rock bottom because at least at rock bottom you are on a rock that can't roll. I went through one of the lowest periods of depression my life had ever seen. Four pastors committed suicide, but if not for the Grace of God, I was almost number five. Thanks to the faithful people God placed around me, like Sister Janis Scott, who connected me with Global Faith Alliance I was able to pick up where I left off, and now the children from our church collect hygiene and health care products, and we are serving the poor and underprivileged people of the islands. I got my second wind, and the people who show up every week to hear me preach the Gospel let me know my voice is still relevant for this generation. I refuse to give up my will. You have a will. Out of all the other things God gave you, He gave you a will. I hear the scriptures saying this is the day the Lord has made, and I *will* rejoice and be glad in it. Job said after trial upon trial, "Though you slay me, *yet will I trust.*" All I am saying is don't lose your will. Maintain your constitution about yourself that says I've got to get a grip. Thank God for the spider.

Now that you have gotten your grip back, you can also recover what you lost.

A Strategy for Recovering Lost Things!

> [8] *Either what woman having ten pieces of silver, if she lose one piece, doth not light a candle, and sweep the house, and seek diligently till she find it?*
>
> [9] *And when she hath found it, she calleth her friends and her neighbours together, saying, Rejoice with me; for I have found the piece which I had lost.*
>
> [10] *Likewise, I say unto you, there is joy in the presence of the angels of God over one sinner that repenteth.*
>
> Luke 15:8–10

Luke 15 is known as the lost and found of the Bible. One man lost a sheep, one man lost a son, and a woman lost a piece of silver. All of us in life at one time or another have lost something of value, perhaps something tangible like this coin, meaning something we can touch. I've lost cars and money and clothes and things that were of some sentimental value, like jewelry and what have you. But then there are some things that are intangible, like joy, peace, love, and friendships—ideas that I waited too long to act upon. Some of us have lost relationships with our children or spouses and have lost intangible things that couldn't be seen or touched with human hands. However, this woman gives us a strategy for recovering lost things. She offers a recipe of sorts and some hope that although some things are out of sight, it doesn't mean they are out of mind.

The story says she had ten pieces of silver, which means she could have easily said, "Don't worry about the one. I've got nine more." But instead, she thought that even that one had some worth and value that it would be more near and dear to her found than forgotten. Aren't you glad we serve a God who values us like that? He wouldn't be satisfied until even the one was found. John Newton caught this concept and wrote in that great hymn of the church, "I once was lost, but now I'm found." Get a revelation that will change your mind. Understand that you matter to God. That's why you are reading this book—God had you on his mind. You are not an afterthought. You are one of His favorites. He will go through any extent to find us. If you are in prison, he found you and wants you to know your CUP size. If you are in the middle of a nasty divorce, let Him fight your battles. What's around us, behind us, and ahead of us is nothing compared to what's inside of us. God will redeem the time. He will make things stop on your behalf.

So what did this woman do? Well, first the Bible says that she lit a candle. That, my sister, is *illumination*. She understood that it was impossible to find anything in the dark, so she had to turn the light on. If you lost something, the quickest way to find it is to use the light of God's word. Anywhere else would be like looking in the dark. He declares that His word is a lamp unto my feet and a light unto my path. Illumination, my sister, is when you come out of the darkness into the marvelous light. Turn the light on. Abuse is dark. Self-hate is dark. Depression is dark, self-pity is dark, and prejudices are dark. Profiling people and prejudging people is dark. Turn the light on.1st John 4:4 says Greater is He that is within me than he that is within the world. That sheds some light. When everything around you says no, He says yes by saying that I can do all things through Christ that strengthens me. That sheds some light. Illumination is discovering that what you lost may be in dark places, but the bigger tragedy is not the losing or the leaving but looking in the dark. Turn the light on by getting some counseling. In this book, I speak about finding a coach. Sometimes you need a coach to help you achieve your goals of recovering what is lost. Turn some light on.

Secondly, the Bible says she swept the house. That was *perspiration*, meaning that this wasn't an easy task for the faint of heart. She swept every nook and cranny. She moved furniture. And I would like to note this was not a marble floor or tile or linoleum. It wasn't the kind of floor you could just go get a Swiffer and run over it and be done. No, it was a dirt floor, and to make matters worse, she had to make her own broom. There was no Wal-mart or dollar store to run to and pick up some cleaning supplies. She had to put her back into it. It required going to cut a tree and then going to get straw and then weaving the straw and binding the top of the straw. I don't know about you, but I got tired just thinking about it. Well, that's the way life is. Some stuff is not going to be a cakewalk. You may have to put some elbow grease into it. I used to resent my father and how seemingly hard he was on me in my youth, but today, I thank God for what he instilled in me, like my work ethic. My mother used to say, "Laziness will kill you." She downright knew I've got to give this all I've got. It's some work. And also sweeping will work up a sweat. And anything worth having is worth sweating for.

Then there was *determination*. The last clause of verse 8 says, "And seek diligently until she find it." She didn't quit. She didn't give up on it. How many folks were determined to keep you and I lifted in prayer although we were lost? Somebody has a loved one who is lost or strung out on drugs. All I say is don't give up on that boy, that girl, that marriage, that degree. Like the woman, we must be determined. Others, no doubt told her to give up on the coin, but I hear her saying, "Nope. I am determined." Something inside of her was resolute without fail. I grew up in the old Baptist Church and they sang a song that said, "What is this? Got me feeling so good right now. What is this? Makes me want to run on anyhow. Whatever it is. It won't let me hold my peace. What is this? Makes people say I'm acting strange. What is this? Makes me wanna run on in Jesus name. Whatever it is. It won't let me hold my peace, and then it would close and say it makes me love my enemies, it makes me love my friends, and it won't let me be ashamed to tell the world I've been born again." The song is called "What is This?" But I believe it's that Godly determination that won't let me throw in the towel on life.

After all of that, she called everyone she could find and said, "Rejoice with me." Now that's a cause for a *celebration*. I've found it now she says, "Let's have a celebration." And that is the victory of every soul that is won to the kingdom: a Heavenly Holy Ghost party. The angels and God throw a party over one soul. It's a big deal. One coin, one soul, one child, one class-mate, one loyal friend, one mentor, one teacher—that one person who makes a difference was and is worth it.

CHAPTER 9

"My Tissue has an Issue-It's You: Issues Women Have"

All of us have some issues. Sometimes it's you. Yep, I hate to rain on your parade. I know I have spent this whole book building you up, so I would not dare tear you down in one chapter, but if you are going to live out loud and know your CUP size, we have to deal with your issue. The breasts are tissue. They are mammary tissue, and they grow and form what we call the breasts. Now this is sensitive because you have to pay attention to what's going on in your body; thus, mammograms are necessary, and then also feeling around this tissue gives you the signs and signals as to what's going on inside of the tissue. I want to suggest that you shouldn't take on a defeatist attitude about your issues in your body. God made you, and whatever He made, He can manage; therefore, if by chance there are issues in our tissues, it doesn't mean punishment and defect. God didn't have a bad day, and no, you are not a mistake, and God is not mad at you and trying to get you back. If that were the case, you would have never woken up. Maybe it's through our issues that God is saying remember first that if it's over your head, it's still under His feet; and then maybe He's prodding and pointing us toward cures and medical breakthroughs because the solution is often in the pollution. We see this ever so clearly in Mark's Gospel where we find a woman with what I call an issue with her tissue.

> 21 And when Jesus was passed over again by ship unto the other side, much people gathered unto him: and he was nigh unto the sea.

> 22 And, behold, there cometh one of the rulers of the synagogue, Jairus by name; and when he saw him, he fell at his feet,

> 23 And besought him greatly, saying, My little daughter lieth at the point of death: *I pray thee*, come and lay thy hands on her, that she may be healed; and she shall live.

> 24 And *Jesus* went with him; and much people followed him, and thronged him.

> 25 And a certain woman, which had an issue of blood twelve years,

26 And had suffered many things of many physicians, and had spent all that she had, and was nothing bettered, but rather grew worse,

27 When she had heard of Jesus, came in the press behind, and touched his garment.

28 For she said, If I may touch but his clothes, I shall be whole.

29 And straightway the fountain of her blood was dried up; and she felt in *her* body that she was healed of that plague.

30 And Jesus, immediately knowing in himself that virtue had gone out of him, turned him about in the press, and said, Who touched my clothes?

31 And his disciples said unto him, Thou seest the multitude thronging thee, and sayest thou, Who touched me?

32 And he looked round about to see her that had done this thing.

33 But the woman fearing and trembling, knowing what was done in her, came and fell down before him, and told him all the truth.

34 And he said unto her, Daughter, thy faith hath made thee whole; go in peace, and be whole of thy plague.

Mark 5:21–34 (KJV)

How to Stop the Bleeding

All of us would agree that bleeding affects us the same way.

When we are bleeding by injury or by sickness, bleeding either suspends or stops us from progressing or finishing whatever we are engaged in. If you are bleeding, it is going to either suspend or stop you to the point that you have to disengage in whatever activity you are engaged in, address the bleeding, and stop it so that you can progress in whatever activity you are engaged in. Simply put, if you don't stop the bleeding, it will stop you.

And I have a sneaky suspicion that there are some bleeding people reading this book, who have not been able to complete an assignment *because* they are bleeding. Many of you have not been able to complete a project because you are bleeding or haven't been able to finish the work God has placed in your hands, whether privately or publicly, because you are bleeding.

So it is, the Word of the Lord is tailored to teach us that you know the bleeding requires for you to give attention to it. It requires for you at some point, to stop what you are doing and give attention to it so that you can be most effective at what God has assigned your hands to do.

Now I have a strange confession before I proceed—I can't stand some church folks because they don't like to disclose where they are bleeding. It becomes our church behavior to hide where we are wounded, so we usher bleeding, we sing bleeding, we preach bleeding, and we serve bleeding when actually you cannot be at your optimum if you don't stop and address the areas where your heart and mind are wounded. It's God's challenge for you today to understand that in order for you to reach your optimum, stop and address the areas where you are wounded.

Such as the discipline discovered in the discourse of Mark 5, our Lord Jesus Christ is in the process of engaging His ministry when He is addressed by one of the rulers of the synagogue. His name is Jairus, and he comes and tells Jesus, "My daughter is in the process of dying. But if you will come and touch her and heal her, she shall live."

Jesus decides, "I'm going to stop my route to Calvary and go by Jairus's house and address his dying daughter." And in the process of going to Jairus's house, He gets a second interruption by a woman who has been bleeding for twelve years. Jesus decides again to address this woman's bleeding, and in the process of this, the Bible says around verse 35 that a messenger comes from Jairus's house and says, "Troublest thou not the master any longer. Your daughter is dead."

I want to suggest, ladies, that it immediately introduces to us the need to address our issues. This text is tailored to teach us—churched or unchurched—that there are some young people who are dying because of grown folks' issues, and it becomes imperative and important that some of you grown people address your issues because the casualties can become the next generation. Your issue is bigger than you, it affects more than just you, and it becomes dangerous to more than just your life, so it becomes imperative that if we are going to save the next generation, we've got to address our current adult issues.

Jesus addresses this woman's issues as He gives attention to her, but it's interesting that Mark records all of the road and route that led to her attention to Christ. She's gone to doctors, and she's spent all she has, and they haven't been able to help her. She finally decided to go touch the hem of Jesus's garment and the Bible says that the fountain of her blood dries up. By the time she gets to Jesus, the passage started out with Him referring to her as "woman," but by the time we get to verse 34, He calls her "daughter." He just didn't heal her, He saved her; and though she started off as just a natural person, Jesus says, "I'm not just going to save you from bleeding, I'm going to wash you in the blood. You're going to be my daughter because I don't just need to heal you; I need to make you one of my children." He means that mainly because you're going to run into some other bleeding people, and I'm going to need somebody with a testimony that God can't only just save you *from* blood, He can save you *with* blood.

That's the story, so let me back up and share some things with you that I think are pertinent to our walk with God and how knowing your CUP size will help you deal with the issues in your tissue.

Ladies, let it be duly noted at the introduction of this text that bleeding is not a sickness. Bleeding is a symptom.

What she's bleeding from is actually left in biblical anonymity, for we don't know what she's bleeding from. All we know is that she's bleeding. Matthew, Luke, and John all have their own record of this woman, and none of them disclose her sickness, they all just discuss her symptoms. She's been bleeding for twelve years, and maybe, ladies and gentlemen, God did not allow them to disclose her sickness to share with us that in life the effects are worse than the cause. Maybe you have to learn to get a grip on the effects because you can be delivered from the cause and still be wrestling with the effects. They only highlight her symptoms. She shares with us that if you are going to stop the bleeding, the first thing you've got to do is *realize the consequences.* The text says that there are physical consequences. She's been bleeding for twelve years, which translates, ladies, that she's been uncomfortable in her own skin.

For twelve years—not twelve *days,* but for twelve *years*—she had struggled to like herself, and for twelve years she had walked around, uncomfortable and discontent in her own skin and in her own body. You know some of you have that same problem because you are only happy when you get other people's approval. But when you are happy in your own skin, you know how to date yourself, you are happy with yourself, you're not waiting on anybody else to celebrate you, you're content in your own skin, you don't compete with anybody, you don't covet anybody, you're not comparing yourself to anybody. You know how to be happy about yourself.

Twelve years she was uncomfortable in her own skin. There were physical consequences but not only are there physical consequences, the Bible says, there are social consequences.

She was struggling with something that is subject to legalities, Leviticus 15 says. Because of her issue, she had to be disconnected from mainstream society, so she has social consequences. If she had a relationship, she could no longer have it because of her issues. If she had children, she could no longer have a healthy relationship with her kids because of her issues. She was disconnected from society. People with issues are *distant people*. They're difficult for people to get along with. They stay away from family. They struggle to socialize. It's not that they are evil, they just don't know how to handle their issues around other people. Now if you say amen, it looks like I'm not talking to you, but if you know somebody in your family or you know somebody on the job who has a struggle socializing, you can usually identify this person because he or she thinks everybody else is crazy and thinks something is wrong with everybody else, but this person doesn't want you to know that he or she is struggling with an issue.

It has physical consequences and social consequences, and it also has financial consequences. The text says she goes broke over her issue. You see, ladies and gentlemen, when you realize that your issues are expensive. You would have more money if you didn't have your issue. You wouldn't be broke right now if it weren't for your issue, and everyone reading this book—including myself, has to realize that your issues are connected to your finances and that your finances are connected to your issues, and if you get hold of your issue, you get hold of your finances.

Realize the consequences. The consequences are physical, social, and financial. Let me sum all that up by saying that issues prohibit us from living a normal life. That's why it's imperative that you stop the bleeding.

You have to realize the consequences but you also have to *restrain from costly choices*. Watch what she says, ladies. This woman actually has two issues.

Her first issue is the issue of blood, but she also has a second issue—and that is an issue of opinions. The text says she goes from doctor to doctor, and every doctor she goes to has another opinion. She has been to doctor after doctor seeking a second and third opinion, and what's making her issue worse is that she's got too many opinions in her spirit.

I believe that's why some of us are dealing with trusting ourselves. Too many times we value others' opinions over and above our own. Now allow me to be clear. I believe doctors are a gift from God. At least some of them are. Yet, you must begin to trust your instincts about your issues sometime. You can go to doctors and specialists all you want, but you live in your body twenty-four hours a day, and that's your earth suit. God equipped us with stuff on the inside to alert us that there may be an issue. Learn to listen to your body. I still argue that maybe you might be up in the air over something that potentially could be small, but you have blown it up because you have too many opinions in your spirit.

> Blessed is the man that walketh not in the counsel of the ungodly, nor sitteth in the seat of the scornful or standeth in the way of sinners but his delight is in the law of the lord and in his word doth he meditate day and night.
>
> Psalms 1:1–2

Your counsel ought to not be from a talk show all the time; it ought to be from the word of God, so stop listening to your girlfriend. She may be very well meaning; however, your family and friends are not always right. I know you've heard from Gerald and Geraldine, but what does God say about it? As a matter of fact, as I write this book, apps are a big deal now. "There's an app for that" has become the newest catchphrase. Allow me to say that whatever your issue, God has an app for it in His Word.

Now, don't miss the main point I just discussed, which is that every opinion is costing her money and time. This is what she would want me to tell you, I believe, if she were alive today. If you are going to stop the bleeding, you first have to stop investing in people who are not making a difference in your life. They just constantly rob you of your investment.

You have to stop investing in these people who, when you look closely, don't make you change for the better, don't help you pray any harder or prosper, or don't help you seek God, but they steadily rob you of your investment. *Refrain from costly choices.*

She's struggling with a physical malady, and she goes to doctor after doctor, and it yields the same outcome. Now, allow me to say I like Mark's account because he is insensitive. Mark is giving me the state of her physical condition when I really ought to be getting this from Luke, who by trade and profession is a physician. Luke 8, by way of his synoptic account, says that she spent all she had on doctors and that they could not heal her. Mark says that's not what happened. Mark says she went to doctor after doctor, and they made it worse. Did you catch that?

I should have been getting this information from Dr. Luke, but Mark says, "I'm not going to hide it because Luke is trying to protect his practice and his profession. I can't let you dog me because it's possible"—and if I may give you what I call the Bondology version—"that Luke could have been one of the doctors she went to." So Luke says, "Let me protect my practice and tell you we couldn't heal her." Mark says, "She went to doctors, and doctors made it worse." Now listen, ladies, because sometimes if you're too spiritual, you miss the revelation of reality in the text. As a woman who knows her CUP size, you have got to be honest enough to admit when some things are not working.

If she was struggling with a physical malady, wasn't she supposed to go to doctors? I mean, after all, when you're sick in your body, you go to the doctor. That makes sense to me. But wait a minute. Mark says she went to doctors, and they made it worse. How do you handle life when you go to the right people and they make it worse? How do you handle life when you go to people you are supposed to go to and the right people make it worse? Can I give you the answer? It wasn't until the doctors failed that she went to Jesus.

Sometimes God will allow the right stuff to go wrong or at least what you thought was the right stuff. Had the doctors worked, she would have never gone to Jesus.

There are times in your life where God will give you successful failure because when it doesn't go right, you will finally go to Jesus. He will let this fail so that you will go find Him; He will let that fall out so that you'll go find Him, and he'll let this mess up so that you'll go find Him.

If you tell the truth, that's when some of y'all start coming to church—when He lets the right stuff go wrong. Now you're at church. You go to Bible study, you read your Word and study, and listen to the gospel music because the right stuff went wrong, and now you want Jesus. There are times when God will let the right stuff go wrong just so you'll go look for Jesus.

I've got the Bible. I'm not making this stuff up. Notice it started out as a random discharge in verse 25; by the time we get to verse 29, it's a fountain—a constant flow. By the time she got to Jesus, it was a plague. Had she found Jesus when it was an issue, it would have never become a plague, but she, like some of us, waited until it got out of control, and now she wants to try Jesus. You'd better get to Jesus when it becomes an issue, and it will never become a plague.

You don't believe me? Verses 25–27 are one sentence. There is no period until the end of verse 27. There are three verses in one sentence, but watch this. It is the key word in verse 27, when she had *heard*. It does not say, "then she heard," it says, "when she had heard"—past perfect tense. It does not say when she went to the doctors and "then she heard." It says she went to the doctors "when she had heard." You missed it.

She didn't wait until she went broke after going to the doctors and now all of a sudden, she wants to find Jesus. She heard about Jesus when she was going to the doctors. She had no doubt in her mind that if she just went to the doctors that everything would be all right, when in all reality, she should have gone to Jesus first, but she made Jesus last. Please don't act like there haven't been times where you made Jesus last. Most people don't look for Him until they run out of control and choices.

When you get done sweating and crying and trying to make it work yourself, that is when people normally want to go find Jesus. However, if you are going to stop the bleeding, you are going to have to realize the consequences and refrain from costly choices. BThird, if you are going to stop the bleeding, you have to reach for Christ. Now, allow me to warn you, my sisters, that her theology doesn't agree with ours. I don't know much about her history or upbringing, so I don't know how she resolves her own healing.

Her language is clear. She declares, "If I may but touch His clothes, I am going to be made whole." I'm not quite sure where she gets this line of reasoning, so the safest thing I could say is that sometimes suffering will cause your theology to surface. Now mind you, she makes her own self-imposition, and it does not agree with our theology. For she says, "If I touch Him, I'm going to be made whole." We normally think if someone touches us or lays hands on us, we will be healed and whole, but she says, "If I could just touch Him." I admire the fact that she didn't wait for Him to touch her, but she reached for Jesus.

Listen, some days, you ought to not go to church and just take a seat and go through the ritual, routine, and regimen; you ought to come in the door reaching for an encounter with him. If you have to come in, go straight to the altar. "You just let the people know I'm not going to be disruptive. Y'all go ahead and sing. Pastor, you go ahead and preach, but I just got to reach for Him, because I don't have time for anyone to lay hands on me. I am here reaching for Him." Like the songwriter declares, "I'm chasing after you."

What I like about this passage is that He did what she said, because He told her, "Your faith has made you whole." Jesus wasn't even in the conversation, according to Pastor Tolan Morgan of Detroit.

God has the power to do it. You must remember that death and life are in the power of the tongue. I dare you to start declaring some things, because if you are bold enough to say it, you are then eligible to seize it. She said what she saw until she saw what she said.

Declare a thing, and it shall be.

Now understand the fact that she had to reach through a crowd, so she had to get down on her knees. And I want to suggest some stuff you can't fight on your feet, but you may have to kneel on your knees. Because if you have more bowing down, you will have less breaking down.

Shockingly He asked a question Jesus says "Who touched me?" I've heard many declare that because of his omniscience, He's all knowing. So He already knows the answer. So why would He ask the question? Allow me to share with you that whenever we have some issues in our tissue and if hH asks a question, He's not looking for the answer; He's looking for attention. She was about to sneak away and not acknowledge or worship for what was done in her life. When sometimes God has to get our attention and alert us so that we will not miss our miracles. Whenever you learn your CUP size and get some issues cleared up, you do not have the right to remain silent. You ought to testify.

The second reason he asked the question was because Jairus was there. And he needed for Jairus to hear her testimony because Jairus just got the news that his daughter had died. Jairus is going to need some faith for what he was getting ready to encounter. He knows that if Jesus can handle this woman's twelve-year-long disease issue, He also could handle his twelve-year-old daughter issue.

There is a woman, a girl, or a female—someone you may not even know—who needs the benefit of hearing you talk about your issues not from a haughty spirit but from a healed perspective. Your story will let some other woman know she's not the only one who has had some issues in her tissue.

I want you to know with pristine precision that God is always on the case. Even if you have to live with some of your issues in your tissue, your CUP size dictates that you can handle it before it handles you. Issues prove humanity, because pain oftentimes reminds us that although you were bleeding, the miracle is that you didn't bleed out and die. You lived with the disease. Now that is the real miracle.

CHAPTER 10

CUP-Size Cash Flow:
How to Master Your Money!

The secret to building wealth in thirty days. The one secret law of becoming a millionaire that they don't want you to know about. Three keys to becoming like the billionaire two doors down. Wow! What alluring language—and eye catching if nothing else. I was caught in a dilemma naming this chapter because it's titles like I aforementioned that catch people's eyes and also titles like these that sell. Yet my integrity and character wouldn't and won't ever allow me to stoop to mind debauchery to trap people into some false sense of euphoria about a subject matter. So here is the truth about the secret to wealth: *the secret is that there is no secret!* Yes, girlfriend, there is no secret. It's about understanding principle and information. I teach very candidly to my audience that if you practice the principle, you will possess the promise.

It's simple. The Bible is a book of promises; however, every promise is preceded by a principle. If you practice the prescribed principle, then the result is the yielding of the promise. Watch this very simple one: "Be thou faithful over a few, and I will make you ruler over much." The four words I want you to extract are the principle (*faithful* and *few*) and then the promise (*ruler* and *much*). Think about it. Why would I give you ten pounds to lift if you couldn't pick up a five-pound weight? But when you can handle and you prove faithful over the smaller amounts of weight, then you can prepare for much, or shall I say increase. I only used weights as an example, but the principle applies in every area of your life. If you can't manage $5, which would be a few, how then can you manage $5 million, which is much?

The second thing I want to convey is that most people remain poor or can never really get to their wealthy places because of ignorance. They need to be exposed to the right information and then be motivated to apply that knowledge to their own individual situations. Now please be mindful that I will share with you very practical and pragmatic ways to, as I say, master your money. I firmly believe that if you don't master it, you will become mastered by it. So let's look at some very common-sense life lessons on how to master your money.

I want to take a moment and offer you loving advice on how to master your money. Money is a tool—a very powerful and popular one at that. Jesus actually talks about money in over half of His parables. "I wish above all things that thou mayest prosper and be in good health as thy soul doth prosper" (3 John 1:2) is just one of many scriptures that speaks about God's desire for us and wealth or prosperity. It seems to suggest that God doesn't mind us having money; He just doesn't want money to have us. You must understand moving forward that we are God's children and He wants what's best for us. That's why the Bible did not say money was the root of all evil—but that the love of it is. Now, you are a woman and you know that women love harder than any creatures on the planet, and when people love a thing, they will do anything for it. God loves us so much that He sent His son to die for us, so love knows no boundaries. As it relates to money, I've seen people do some very heinous and even criminal things to get it—kill, steal, cheat, lie—you name it. We must understand how we are to think about and view money:

Number one: money is first in your mind. You must have the right mindset about money or you will never have any. Second, you won't know how to handle it when you acquire it. Third, you will resent people with money. Let's take a moment to deal with your mind's view on money because the Bible says people are destroyed for the lack of knowledge. One version says this:

> 6 My people are ruined because they don't know what's right or true. Because you've turned your back on knowledge, I've turned my back on you priests. Because you refuse to recognize the revelation of God, I'm no longer recognizing your children.
>
> Hosea 4:6 (MSG)

What powerful language the above scripture displays. If you dig the well of truth, it is referring to a group who were not void of knowledge, but rather who chose to avoid the knowledge available. To be ignorant means to be "*ignore*-ant," meaning that sometimes we choose to ignore what's available. Whether you subscribe to Christianity or not, this is true regardless of race, age, or ethnicity. It doesn't matter. If you have an ignorant or an impoverished mind-set about money, then you will have destruction or ruin. I love the quote by David Livingstone who says, "I will go anywhere as long as it's forward." So let's get your mind right first. As they say, "Let's get rid of that stinking way of thinking."

Let me pause and say that if you clear up your mind and change your mind, then you change your money capacity. In the wonderful book *Secrets of the Millionaire Mind*, T. Harv Eker does a wonderful job discussing what he calls your "money blueprint." (I told you there were no secrets, because if it were, he wouldn't have put it in a book). No house, building, or structure gets built without a set of blueprints. This is the plan, but planning doesn't start on paper; it starts in the mind. I want to challenge you to broaden your money mentality. You first must master your mind-set and beliefs and thoughts about money before you master your money. Eker states the very first principle that millionaires understand, and that is this: "Your income can only grow to the extent you do!" So I first challenge you to expose yourself to people who have and handle money. As I said in an earlier chapter, get away from people who have your problem, and get around people who have your answer. Allow yourself to be exposed and stretched by someone who is masterful as it relates to money. How many wealth-management friends do you have in your cell phone Rolodex? How many wealth-creation experts do you socialize with? Let me give you a hint they don't hang out at the mall. Expand your inner, and then your outer will begin to change. Go digging for the knowledge—it's available all around you. If you lock yourself up in a prison of minuteness, you will live in the living room and not be aware that there are other rooms in the house. Stop limiting yourself to consumerism. If you want to be wealthy, do what wealthy people do—don't ignore the knowledge. Information can change your situation. Being exposed gives you options, and when you have options, you can make informed decisions.

For instance, have you ever done something and then later on someone comes along and says something you didn't know? You say, "Well, if I had known that, I would have done something else instead." That's simply saying that if you had been exposed to that piece of information and knowledge, it would have affected your decision. Plainly put, expand your mind and your money will expand, as well.

Number two: in what direction are you sending your money? Clearly, you must have somewhere for your money to go, or you will look up and wonder where it went. Money, like children, needs direction. A part of determining your CUP size is knowing first what it is. If your outgoing exceeds your income, then your upkeep will be your downfall. You must have a place for your money to go. All I have to do is look at your budget, and it will tell me where your money went without you having to say a word. There is an old saying that says, "A fool and her money soon part." Well, let's reverse that ideology. The way you do that is to be honest about where your money is going. You have to have a destination on purpose for your money, remember money is a tool in your hands. As an avid lover of all types of music, particularly Al Green. He and a lady named Ann Nesby have a song entitled "Put It on Paper." It's a love song about a woman who is in a relationship with a man, and they obviously love each other, but there is one problem: they are not married. There is an urging from one or the other that they need to make it official and stop playing house and going through the motions of doing what married couples do and go downtown and get some license and put it on paper. In other words, make it official. In the old church I grew up in, they called it "shacking" when a couple wasn't legally married. So here is my question: If you don't have a budget, are you married to your money or shacking?

If you have a healthy relationship with your finances, then put it on paper and have a purpose and a direction for it to go, or again, you will look up and wonder where it has gone. Often, when I counsel people as it relates to finances or I am in a group teaching on this subject matter, I will call on a random person in the audience and ask her to cup her hands together side by side as tight as she can and then I will fill her hands with water and walk away and continue to teach. Well, after a while, I come back and ask the person for the water, and she says every time, "I tried to hold on to it, but it seeped through the cracks of my hands until slowly but surely it was all gone." Well, that's the way your money is if you don't have a purpose and a place for it, girlfriend. It will eventually seep and slip through your fingers, and you will wonder, "Where did my money go?"

Number three: always invest forward. We all have things we like because we are different. We are so different that some people this morning took baths, some took showers, some washed up really well, and some people didn't do anything because we are different. Because we are different, some people this morning had coffee, some had a bagel, some people ate a full-course meal, and some people didn't eat anything because we are different. Because we are different, some people set out to get married in life. Some women like 'em tall, dark, and handsome; some women like 'em short, fat, and ugly. Some women don't care how he looks as long as he has some money. Some people will work for a living. Some people will spend all their money and borrow yours; some people are so cheap that they will squeeze a dollar until the eagle hollers, but whatever the case, all of us are different, surprisingly we all share one trait: we all have things we like or that give us pleasure. They are what I've described earlier in the book as creature comforts, like cash, cars, clothes, cribs, and cruises. There is nothing wrong with spoiling yourself and—the new term—some retail therapy. However, these are not investments. Investments are things that yield a return, whether tangible or intangible; thus, it is of the utmost importance to invest forward. What are you setting aside for a rainy day? Are you living paycheck to paycheck? Do you have a 401(k) or a Roth IRA? These are things and terms that any woman who knows her CUP size must answer. Now don't be discouraged—Here's a little formula that you can apply immediately upon your next pay period or increase increment:

Sample Budget

You made $1,300 this week or biweekly. Put 10 percent toward tithes/charity, 10 percent to yourself in some form of savings or investment fund, and then the rest in order of your necessities. For example rent/mortgage; then car note, insurance, gas; and then food and groceries (I'm sure you've figured out that you cannot eat out every day and get ahead). Then pay off any outstanding debts, credit cards and as you pay them off, shred them.

This would be the ideal time to minimize some overhead. Now, I know you have some things you think you absolutely can't live without, but let's be realistic—do you actually need 350-plus channels of cable? You can't watch but one channel at a time, and if you are honest, you are really not at home that much that you need four Showtime and five HBO and four Cinemax channels. You really only watch about five to ten channels anyway, so it might be time to go to a basic package or ask your cable rep for a cheaper bundle package for your internet, cable, and phone, then you can save that extra thirty to forty bucks a month.

Second, do you have to eat out every day? When was the last time you packed a lunch for about thirty days? You would be surprised at how much you could save. Do you actually need a new outfit or pair of shoes every weekend? You can't wear but one outfit at a time; you can't wear but one pair of shoes at a time. My point is to trim the fat and fluff where you can.

Then there are ways of getting ahead. I'm not saying reduce yourself to meager peasantry, but stop trying to live above your means and impress people. It may not be feasible to drive an Escalade right now—get a car for cash that runs well and is dependable. It may not be feasible to live in a condo uptown right now—go get a roommate and split the cost in a safe place in midtown. Curb your online and shopping habits, and start mixing and matching some of the clothes you already own. Dig through that closet, and make two piles. One pile is for stuff you can fit in and wear, and start rearranging and recoordinating and revising some of the throwback outfits. Trust me, they will never know the difference. The other pile is stuff you can sell to a consignment shop or on eBay or Amazon and use to start your nest egg. All I am saying is all of your money shouldn't be on your back and in your driveway. Invest forward. And remember, Suze Orman says it this way: "The best way to get out of a hole is to stop digging."

You may not like me now, but you will love me later.

I told you that I love music. In addition, I am also a movie fan. Several years ago Oprah Winfrey produced a movie called *The Great Debaters*, and in the film, there is a scene where the preacher and his son were in the living room of their home. The son, like most kids, wanted to rush out to play or go out for some recreation. The father, played by Forest Whitaker, was a very strict disciplinarian who asked his son in an accountable manner if he had done his chores and studies. The son had a look of sadness on his face, and after he dropped his head, the father reminded him of the household mantra and asked him to recite it outloud. The son replied, "We do what we have to do now so we can do what we want to do later." My point is to do what you have to do now so that you can do what you want to later. So when I say to stop living above your means, I'm simply saying, "Let me see your stability, not your blingability."

In kingdom economics, you see money slightly differently because it is not only tool but also is seed. A seed is nothing but a harvest with potential. The Bible says as long as the earth shall remain, there shall be seed time and harvest. Genesis 8:22 (KJV) says, "While the earth remaineth, seedtime and harvest; and cold and heat, and summer and winter, and day and night shall not cease." Understand as a woman who knows her CUP size, you must be a sower and a saver. CUP-size women are sowers. Why? Because you understand that he giveth seed to the sower.

Stingy people never succeed. I'm not saying that you should give everything away, but understand your ability to pay it forward and pass it on. Learn how to handle money, not hoard money. Part of the proper handling of money is to be a conduit of resources. A conduit is a pipe in which things are channeled and pass through. You can get more in an open hand than a closed and clinched fist. This is how they catch wild monkeys in Africa. Wild monkeys love coconut, so the hunter digs a hole and makes it wide enough for the monkey to get his hand in the top, and the hunter pours concrete around the top of the hole's opening and puts coconut shavings and juice and seeds down in the hole. The monkey comes and sticks his hand in the hole and grabs a handful of the coconut shavings, and because his hand is full, it's stuck, and the monkey is trapped. In order to get free, all the monkey has to do is open his hand and let go of what's in it. Sometimes, in order to be free, you have to learn to let go of what's in your hand, and that doesn't have to always be money; it can be power, control, or information that can help someone get ahead. There was a song by Kenny Rogers in the '70s about gambling, and he said, "You got to know when to hold 'em and know when to fold 'em." So, know when to save and know when to sow. A seed can break the back of poverty in your life. There have been people who have sown into my life and made this book possible, and as they've sown into me, I'm sowing into you. I encourage you to grasp this ideology, because you want to sow where you want to go. Find a money mentor, and stop speaking negative words over your present financial state and decree and declare, "I am not broke. I'm just between blessings."

Financial Discipline

"And when he had spent all, there arose a mighty famine in that land; and he began to be in want."

—Luke 15:14 (KJV)

Financial discipline is an area that most Americans struggle with, but as a woman who knows her CUP size, you need to know how to master your money. The first time I appeared on the Trinity Broadcasting Network (TBN), I discussed money in the hands of believers; especially in the face of a failing economy and at the height of the recession. To their dismay, I humbly submitted that the recession was good because America had become intoxicated on wastefulness and overindulgence. I also said that it was time for the faithful to learn how to be frugal, because I believed that many Christians didn't have a money problem; they had a management problem.

I want to just list a few helpful hints on this subject matter. I believe that all of us recognize the fact that individuals who have matriculated in the halls of higher academia have left those different universities and colleges with a plethora of different skills, but one skill that many didn't leave with is how to handle their money.

You can learn in school all about algebra. They will teach you all about psychology and sociology, and you can even graduate with a PhD and not even know how to balance a checkbook. The world is filled with millions of educated people who pursue their professions successfully but later find themselves struggling financially. You may have experienced it personally where you work harder but can't seem to get ahead. Many follow the age-old advice of their parents that simply said get an education, get married, find a job, climb the corporate ladder, make a lot of money, buy a nice house, have a few children, and retire to live happily ever after. But they discover that "happily ever after" is an elusive place.

There's so much anxiety in our world because most people don't have any financial discipline. Most of us can't seem to get out of the rat race where we are running through a maze for cheese, but the problem I have with that is—only rats settle for cheese. At what point do we realize that life is more than a higher-floor condo; a flat screen in every room, and a traffic jam in the driveway? It burdens my heart even more when I see people by the millions going as far as to drive across state lines to take a chance at winning the lottery. If only they knew that the lottery is defined as a wager levied against people who can't read, meaning that the basic idea is you have to make a whole lot of losers just to have one or two winners. While researching lottery online at dictionary.com I discovered an 1878 Supreme Court opinion held that lotteries had "a demoralizing influence upon the people"—plainly put, the lottery gives people with no idea of wealth management, a false hope of something they couldn't handle because if they were thinkers, they would not waste resources on it.

There are some who even lie in wait of hopes that a rich uncle may die and leave them an inheritance, but even in the educational experience, what's missing is how to handle money properly. We're motivated to make money, but we have no one to show us how to spend it properly or save it wisely. It's normally too late to teach people who are not money savvy how to get money to work for them instead of having them working for it. Without financial discipline, most people will find themselves in a life that is financially shipwrecked, so for those who are going downhill fast—pump your breaks, and with a few minor adjustments, you may find out that you have more discipline than you would have thought. I remember the simplicity of those age-old adages that my father used to teach. He used to constantly drill in our heads and our hearts that it's not what you make—it's what you manage. He also taught that money won't spoil—so make sure you put some up.

The first step is a reality check. Maybe you are reading this book and you are what we used to call in the country "well off." Maybe you're two months paid up on your mortgage, your cars are owned and paid off free and clear; the kids are in college and have scholarships, so you can boast and brag about the good life. However, before you break your arm patting yourself on the back, allow me to remind you that just one turn in life's events—one accident, one crisis can put you right back in a place where you can't make ends meet.

We need to learn the principles, precepts, and posture of financial discipline. I know there is a need for our lives to be transformed in this area when I look at the trends and statistics on what women spend money on. I think about the fact that we spent $3 billion in the last ten years on fake hair, nails, and other beauty supply products that eventually went in the trash can. We literally threw $3 billion in the garbage can by spending it on dead stuff. This lets me know that we need a money management metamorphosis, and the only way we're going to change is through financial discipline. Proverbs 25:28 says this in two of my favorite translations.

> 28 He that *hath* no rule over his own spirit *is like* a city *that is* broken down, *and* without walls.

Proverbs 25:28 (KJV)

> 28 A person without self-control is like a house with its doors and windows knocked out.

Proverbs 25:28 (MSG)

The writer says if you lack self-control and discipline, then you are like a city that has been left defenseless and open to all kinds of attacks and is exposed to all kinds of temptations. We must have discipline over our bodies and our blessings. People are quick to call on God for blessings, but perhaps you've been blessed and weren't wise with what you've already been entrusted with.

It's Not All *Your* Fault!

We live in a culture that really doesn't promote discipline. As a matter of fact, people who save their money are called crazy by people who don't. There is this mentality among the younger generation that says YOLO— an acronym for "You only live once." Although that is factual in reality, it is dangerous in misled theory. I would rather be called a stingy, cheap miser and be among the haves than to spend it all and have nothing to show for it but a place among the have-nots. Culturally, it's all about show-and-tell. Name-brand this and name-brand that; and one person has it who can afford it and now all of the friends in that circle are trying to catch up. When I look at 1 Timothy 4:7, it says to exercise yourself for the purpose of Godliness. That goes in an undisciplined person's ear and out the other. It's interesting, the word "discipline" in the Greek is the word "gymnizo," from which our English words "gymnastics," "gymnasium," and "gymnast" are derived. If you have ever watched a gymnast, you already know that it takes skill and discipline to gain that level of control over one's own body. Likewise, if you exercise no restraint; that green bill (or whatever color your currency is) will make you act a fool, even before you get it. In America, many cannot wait until tax time, and when they get their refunds, usually, the money is spent before they open the envelope.

Learn from Others' Mistakes

So, the question is, do you really want to do better? If so, let's look at this young man in Luke 15 briefly and see if he can help guide us around some financial pitfalls.

> [11] And he said, A certain man had two sons:

> [12] And the younger of them said to *his* father, Father, give me the portion of goods that falleth *to me*. And he divided unto them *his* living.

> [13] And not many days after the younger son gathered all together, and took his journey into a far country, and there wasted his substance with riotous living.

> [14] And when he had spent all, there arose a mighty famine in that land; and he began to be in want.

> [15] And he went and joined himself to a citizen of that country; and he sent him into his fields to feed swine.

> [16] And he would fain have filled his belly with the husks that the swine did eat: and no man gave unto him.

> [17] And when he came to himself, he said, How many hired servants of my father's have bread enough and to spare, and I perish with hunger!

> [18] I will arise and go to my father, and will say unto him, Father, I have sinned against heaven, and before thee,

> [19] And am no more worthy to be called thy son: make me as one of thy hired servants.

> Luke 15:11–19 (KJV)

Luke begins at verse 11 by saying that there was a certain man who had two sons; and one day, the younger of the two came and asked for his portion of goods. In modern-day terms, he was asking for his inheritance.

First of all, not to attack the young man, but I believe he represents a majority of the populous as it relates to his mentality. He asked for something he wasn't quite ready for yet. The one thing that has ruined this generation is that we give them things that they are not mature enough to handle much too soon. If you notice, he left home saying, "Give me," but he came back saying, "Make me." According to Old Testament law, the boy would have gotten one-third of the estate, and the oldest son would have gotten two-thirds of the estate to take care of the mother and any unwed sisters, yet this young man was so selfish that he lacked patience. Always train your children that money management requires moderation and patience. My father used to say that the stuff at the mall was made to sell, not buy.

So the young man got too much too soon. I say this to parents of this generation: please don't ruin your children with the mentality of you wanting them to have it better than you had it. That's good, but that shouldn't equate to throwing money at them to buy things to make up for lost time and planting the seed that spending money on them is your way of saying "I love you." They would much rather have you than the things. We have not made our children appreciative of what life has to offer because we feel pressured to keep them entertained, so they go from one tablet screen to the next phone game and media source—so much so that our children don't even know how to communicate anymore. When we get in the car, the vehicles now come with DVD players and screens in the headrest so that when we are in transit, you have to put a movie on. It has killed their ability to notice their surroundings. There is no regard for the beauty of the trees or the ambiance of a blue sky because they are engulfed in the entertainment.

I was in the Caribbean on a mission trip, and we took a break to tour the island. In a gift shop, the women were making their own dyes and materials to sell their crafts, and it was interesting to see them doing everything by hand. A woman passed by me with her son—who couldn't have been any more than twelve—behind her, and he was on a phone playing a game, and he was so engulfed in the game that he almost ran into a display. We ended up at the checkout line together with them in front of me, and he never looked up. I asked the mother, "Are you here on business or for pleasure?"

She said, "We're here on a family vacation."

I was blown away by the fact that his parents brought him to another country that is nothing less than paradise, and he was so engulfed in a video game that he did not even hear his mother call his name. At his age, had my parents been able to afford to bring me to another country, I would have been flabbergasted yet this goes to show you that we are living in an age where this generation has no appreciation, and we constantly make the mistake of not making them earn it because there is something different about what you have to purchase with money you had to work for.

Mistake number two: he went to a far-off country, which was both good and bad. He avoided guidance, but his next mistake was worse. He spent all his money on riotous living. That simply means living without restraint. And the next verse says that not many days thereafter, he began to be in want. Notice that waste always comes before want.

I want to say this to someone who can attest with me that whatever you waste today you always want later. What a sad reality, but it's true. If you waste an education one day, you'll want it later. If you waste an opportunity, you will want it the next day. If you waste your body, you will want it one day. Remember, want always follows waste. Famine always follows feast, scarcity always follows spending, and poverty follows pleasure. All for what? He went from living high on the hog to eating with the hogs.

The next words seem like torture or adding insult to injury. Right after his money ran out, there arose a famine, and no man gave unto him. When the money ran out, all of his friends ran too.

What do you do when no man will give unto you? The Bible says he joined himself to a citizen of that country and took a job in the hog pen and was tempted to eat the husks or the slop that the hogs ate. He became a rebel against his religion because Jews had nothing to do with swine. Then to make matters worse, he basically became a slave. He's been reduced to prostituting himself and his services to the highest bidder, and then he's so low that he almost settles for slop.

My point to you, my sister, is that when you lack discipline and you reject wisdom and you want too much too soon and are not ready for it, you basically end up in the same predicament as the young man. You end up in a world that uses you up and spits you out and then refuses to give you a handout or a hand up, and now you find yourself in financial ruin, working a job that you hate, and compromising your dignity and settling for slop. When I was a kid, my father was a hog-and-cattle farmer, so slopping pigs is something I know all too well, but the way we gathered slop for our hogs was, we would go behind the restaurants to get all the scraps and discarded food that people didn't want; the bus boys would scrape all of it into this barrel, and we would go pick it up in my dad's old pickup truck. It stunk and was often soured from sitting in the sun for hours, but the hogs ate it like it was caviar. My point is this: you are better than settling for everyone else's leftovers.

How to Recover from the Fall

The text says that the man came to himself almost suggesting that he was under some kind of spell, and he was. He was under the spell of the enemy that all of us fall for when we are younger and think we are invincible and that everybody is our friend. He woke up one day and found that all the people he used to ride around in his Escalade chariot (if I may use contemporized terms) wouldn't even give him a ride. The people he used to go to the bars with, and set everybody up on the house with drinks—those same people passed him by and wouldn't even wave. Now he had a great epiphany. He came to himself, which means that he woke up. Then the Bible says, "He said," so he spoke up. Then he thought up, because he said, "How many hired servants of my father have bread and enough to spare, and I perish with hunger?" Verse 18 says, "He said, 'I will arise,'" so that means that he got up. He recognized that where he had landed was a low place that was beneath him, and he said, "I'm going home." So he went home, and he fessed up and said to his father, "I messed up, but if you will give me another chance, I don't mind working my way up from the bottom."

As you walk in the newness of knowing your CUP size, always remember that you,too, can turn your financial situation around. If financial discipline is an area you are deficient in, then do what this boy did. It's never too late to wake up. Wake up and smell the coffee of a brand-new day. There's no time like the present. Wake up and see that there is more available to you than what meets the eye. God's will for you is not to attend Hog Pen University. Wake up, wake up, wake up, wake up, wake up, wake up, wake up. Then speak up. Open your mouth, and start declaring, "I am a child of the king. I am a child of God. I have the favor of God working in my life and on my life and through my life. I am a success story. I am a financially responsible and fiscally frugal human being." Then I challenge you to get up. Get up from a struggling barely making it, land of lack mentality and go for the gold. You are not a debt monger, but you are delivered, and I decree it so.

Daddy Will Handle the Rest

I believe that I am most impressed with the attitude of the father. The Bible says that, when the son was a far ways off, the father spotted him and ran and fell on His neck, which, in our language, simply means that he ran and embraced him and basically was so overwhelmed that he pulled him to the ground. Now, this means the father broke the law because older men never were supposed to run to younger men in that day. Well, God is waiting on us to come back, and He's willing and able and waiting to embrace us likewise. The most spellbinding thing happened next, which was that his father didn't want to discuss his past. Even though he had his little speech rehearsed, the father couldn't have cared less, which tells me that when people are truly repentant, we must stop trying to throw their past back in their faces. We must take on the attitude of the father, which was that he was so glad that his son was back that he didn't want to look back. He was more concerned about restoration. If you will allow me to use contemporized terminology, his father did three things, he said, "Bring me a robe, a ring, and some Reeboks." They all symbolized what the boy was going to need on his road to recovery. He said to bring a robe because, in their culture, slaves were bare chested. No doubt, this boy had literally lost his shirt in the far country and the father didn't want him mistaken as a slave, so he wanted him covered. All my CUP-size queens, you need to be covered. You are not a slave, so make sure you find you some financially astute person to cover you in the financial realm. It may be your pastor or it may take calling Schwab or ING and making an appointment to go sit down with a specialist to discuss your financial future during a free consultation.

Second, the father said to bring a ring. In those days, the rings people wore had insignias on them like a seal that bore the family crest. Well, it was more than a ring; it was also the way they bought groceries and the way they purchased land and signed contracts and worked business deals. It was basically the credit card of their day. So, the father said, "Restore his credit rating."

What never ceases to amaze me is when people ask me about helping to repair or restore their credit, which is one of our businesses, the first thing that I ask them is, "Where is your credit report, and whom do you owe, and what is your score?" In many cases, they don't know, or they just say,

"My credit is bad." Well, how bad? The rule of thumb is know who you owe. I challenge you. Unlike this boy whose credit was restored instantly, I challenge you to work on restoring your credit—not so you can go get more stuff, but so you won't have to be held at bay by these crooked merchants and credit card companies who work at beating you out of all your money with high interest rates and fees. Work on your credit.

And lastly, his father said, "Bring my son some shoes." In those days, you couldn't wear shoes on someone else's land because shoes showed signs of ownership. WHis father wanted him to be able to walk like a privileged landowner, not a peasant or plantation worker, because slaves couldn't wear shoes, period. He also wanted everyone to know that this boy was not a slave; he was a son.

As a woman who knows her CUP size, you are not a slave nor a slouch. Master your money so that you won't be subject to a land of lack; choose rather to walk in a place of plenty. Daddy's waiting on you.

CHAPTER 11

Finding the Right BRA: One Size Really Doesn't Fit All

When bras were first developed in the early 19th century, they were simply undergarments that provided strong support for women's breasts; preventing problems like sagging breasts and backaches. Today, designers and manufacturers worldwide have added to the value of the bra by offering women close to twenty different styles to fit their needs. Here are just a few. Now bare with me, sistas. This may take a minute because you have the advantage on me here, and truthfully speaking, you can't give a man too many choices:

First, allow me to say as we step into the undergarment department that I feel kinda awkward, but also right at home. I called my momma and asked if I was a breast-fed baby. She laughed and said, "Before you left the hospital you were, but that was forty years ago. I was not expecting you and so, by the time I got to you"—(I was child number seven)—"I was tired, and they were coming out with all these formulas that were already mixed."

I said all that because I wanted to know if my earliest experiences with this anatomical part have anything to do with why I am a single Christian male who loves going by Victoria's Secret occasionally and am obsessed with this subject (Confession is good for the soul but bad for the reputation. Note to self 1/3/14 cebj). So as we navigate this section, you will find explanation and inspiration for your expectation of this exploration, because BRA is really an acronym for the three types of people you need in your circle. Mainly, a bra has three main purposes, and so will the people who you will attract on your journey:

B stands for Builders

R stands for Reciprocators

A stands for Affirmers

Builders

Let's begin with B in BRA, which stands for *builders*. This is so foundational for where God is taking you. I've been told that every woman has her three favorite bras. Well, these are in your new fave file. Yes, my sister, you need some builders, not busters and not breakers. Like Gladys Knight said, you've had your share of those. However, builders are your support bras—the ones you can count on who won't let you down (figuratively and literally). The way you find a good builder bra is its expansiveness to be what you need when you need it at different stages and phases. It can get you started and then finish with you, but its main job is to be support at whatever level you are. My old grandmother used to say, "If folks aren't about what you are about, then you don't need to be about 'em." Simply put, your support bra, people, understands their place and space in your life and are not intimidated when where you are does not include them. They are not in it as long as there's a payoff or if it benefits them. They can support silently. They are such builders until they are content to let you shine and are glad to be extras in your movie. They know that you couldn't have done it without them and know that when you make it to the big screen, you won't forget to put their names in the credits. So, as we look at each kind of builder bra, keep in mind to take care of your builders because they are your foundation, folks, and you've got to stand on their shoulders.

> Training bra: this type of bra is designed for preteen or teenage girls who are in the early stages of breast development. It is smaller than standard bra sizes, and its cups come without underwire support. Aside from providing some measure of breast support, it helps young girls to become accustomed to wearing a bra.

Well, can I be honest? Every woman needs this in her life experience, because if you are going to live out loud, you first must get the hang of it. You need a training bra person—someone to show you the ropes. It must be someone who knows where you are and understands that they need to be patient, because at this phase, this is all new. Training bra people understand the awkwardness of this time in your life and that setting the stage is most important. They are the encouragers because they know you are watching the other girls, and some of them are fast developers. They can whisper in your ear, "Take your time, baby. You'll get there." They know that you don't have to stay where you start, yet you gotta start somewhere. You need that trainer, because it's first. It gets you started. It becomes your mental model. Everyone—male and female, has a mental model. This is the person who you patterned after, even when you didn't realize it; and now you do stuff most like them because in your mind you always revert back to how they did it. You saw momma do it, so you do it like momma did it. But a wise training bra person will push you into your own so that you won't feel like you need to be where the other girls are.

> Full-cup bra: This bra provides full support, as it comes with underwired cups and covers most of the breasts. It is recommended for all women, especially for those with heavier breasts.

This is the next builder bra person you need—someone full of wisdom who knows how to cover you and contain you. This needs to be someone who is mature. You cannot have too many full cup bra people who are eye level with you. They need to be someone with some seasoning and some sage because they have a twofold assignment—to cover and contain, thus the underwire. Not only do they cover you up, they hold you up. Do you remember when Noah got drunk? Oh, did I shock you? Well, if you didn't know, now you do—Dr. Pastor Noah had a chemical dependency problem. And the Bible says this:

> 18 And the sons of Noah, that went forth of the ark, were Shem, and Ham, and Japheth: and Ham *is* the father of Canaan.

> 19 These *are* the three sons of Noah: and of them was the whole earth overspread.

> 20 And Noah began *to be* an husbandman, and he planted a vineyard:

> 21 And he drank of the wine, and was drunken; and he was uncovered within his tent.

> 22 And Ham, the father of Canaan, saw the nakedness of his father, and told his two brethren without.

> 23 And Shem and Japheth took a garment, and laid *it* upon both their shoulders, and went backward, and covered the nakedness of their father; and their faces *were* backward, and they saw not their father's nakedness.

> 24 And Noah awoke from his wine, and knew what his younger son had done unto him.

> 25 And he said, Cursed *be* Canaan; a servant of servants shall he be unto his brethren.

> 26 And he said, Blessed *be* the LORD God of Shem; and Canaan shall be his servant.

²⁷ God shall enlarge Japheth, and he shall dwell in the tents of Shem; and Canaan shall be his servant.

Genesis 9:18-27 (KJV)

Well, Noah's son, Ham came in and saw his father drunk and rushed out to expose Noah and tell his brothers. The older two brothers walked in backward so as not to see their father's shame, and they covered him with a sheet.

Girlfriends, people who want to expose you and gossip and tell all your business are not full cup bra material. If a dog will bring a bone, it will carry a bone, but full-cup-bra builder-type people will be the people who will cover you and your shortcomings, not lie for you or be without integrity. They will cover you when you can't cover yourself because they see the potential in you, and they know when you sober up from being drunk on your own wine that God still has a plan for you. You still have an ark to build, and they will cover you and contain you until you get sober.

> Demicup bra: A demicup bra covers only half the breasts, with its cups coming up above the nipples. This bra is suitable to wear with clothes that have plunging necklines. It is supportive yet provides maximum exposure of the breasts.

This type of builder bra person doesn't require much because it knows how to do just the right amount for its assignment. It covers only half, yet it's the most important half. The nipple is the tip that acts as the exit point for what's inside. Not only that, it's where all of the nerve endings congregate. Your demicup-bra people are your balance people—they know that you have to be sane in order to live out loud, so they shield your essentials so that you won't suffer nerve damage. Plainly put, they protect you from what I call the Ator family. Demicup bra people tell Mr. and Mrs. Aggravator that today is not the day. They tell their cousin, Agitator, that she's about to make you take off your earrings. They tell brother and sister Instigator, to mind their own damn business; and well, you know the rest. They let people know where to get off.

> Padded bra: This bra comes with padding inside the cup linings, adding volume to smaller breasts. Padded bras are popular with teenage girls, who may otherwise stuff their training bras with tissues to make their breasts look fuller.

Padded-bra people are significant in this building-bra repertoire. They are the people you can land on something soft when the Ator family called in their grandma Irritator. They know when you're sensitive and can provide the confidence and comfort that are needed in those rough places. They put the proverbial booster cables on you and let you know it's okay to be proud and shake what your momma gave you. When you need that added boost of confidence, they get in your ear and reassure you that we all need a little help sometimes. Don't be ashamed of your goods. Be proud, and don't be intimidated. She'll say, "How are you going to let a nickel tell you that you're not worth a dime?" And before you know it, she ran up your real estate value.

> Underwired bra: bras can come with or without underwire in their cups. An underwired bra provides strong support to the breasts and also maintains the shape of the bra. Some women claim that underwired bras lift their breasts, while others find these bras uncomfortable or painful.

I saved this one for last in the builder-bra section because, although it's becoming less popular, there is still a need to not discount its significance. I've heard many women allude to the fact that this is an uncomfortable bra. However, think with me for a moment. Sometimes the things that make us a little uncomfortable are necessary for the journey. Remember, everything has purpose. All your builder-bra people do not need to be yes-men and yes-women or support your every cause. You need some builders who know how to hold you accountable. It may not feel the best, but they do their job. I'm not the pastor, leader, and life coach I am today because of all my friends and fans, but also because of my foes and my fighters. They are the underwire. Although you didn't always see it and it was a little uncomfortable at times, it was also what helped hold me up because it was a part of the base. Thank God for my underwire bra people.

Reciprocators

Now, this bra, unlike the builders *who represent your foundation*, represents people who hold the responsibility of being your gatekeepers *of flexibility*. Part of being a woman who knows her CUP size is that you must be flexible. David was flexible enough to put on a tux and go calm down an angry savage, Saul with his harp and then go put on his shepherd's overalls and be among nasty, stinky sheep. He had the flexibility to conduct himself in the palace and the pasture and do both with distinction.

Girlfriend, put your big-girl panties on, because you've got to have builder-bra people for your foundation, but you need reciprocators for your flexibility. These are the bra like people who are flexible enough to move with you. They reciprocate or reflect what's needed in the moment. These are the people who help you hold it down because they adjust well. They are like chameleons—they become what they are around. Flexibility is a strength you are going to need to master, because, as women, you are going to be placed in predicaments that will range from easy to extreme, but you've got some bras that can handle it.

> Strapless bra: strapless bras come with no straps or straps that can be removed. This style is very useful for clothes that bare shoulders, such as tube dresses and halter tops.

Now, I started with strapless bra people for the obvious reasons. These are the people who are confident enough in who they are to hold you up incognito. They can get into stealth mode and operate like an usher at church who spots a need, and passes you a fan, or shows you to your seat with a smile and a curtsy. Or they are the people who are like the wedding coordinator/planner—they operate behind the scenes of your life to make you look good because they know this is your day and not theirs, and they are willing to look bad so you don't have to worry about the details. You need some strapless bra people. They are flexible.

> Convertible bra: this bra comes with detachable straps that can be arranged according to one's needs. It is usually worn with clothes that reveal the back and shoulders, such as backless dresses with halter top necklines.

When I was a kid, I loved cars. I admired the old-school cars, and I loved the newer-model sports cars, but nothing said class to me like a convertible. It was the coolest car on the road. It made a statement without saying a word. I most admired it because the convertible was not topless. The top was there, but the onlooker could not see it. It was tucked away in a compartment for when it was needed, like in case of rain or if it got too cold; but it was content to know that it was just as much a part of the car as the engine. Well, you need convertible-bra people who adjust to the outfit or the weather of your life and are content to not be seen, but they are still there. These are the people who may live out of state but are still as close as a phone call away. Your convertible-bra people know what to reveal and what to conceal. They know how to keep a secret and won't judge you because your halter top is revealing.

T-shirt bra: T-shirt bras are made without a raised seam in order to appear invisible when worn under a body-fitting T-shirt.

Now T-shirt-bra people are interesting because these are the people who know how to be visible enough so that you know they are there, yet they complement the outer garment. These people are the people you need to supplement what you already have. They can be counted or counted on— it doesn't make them much difference. They know that if you haven't called them or vice versa for two years, it's okay because you just pick back up where you left off. I love these type of bra people because they are low maintenance.

Minimizer bra: this bra is commonly sought after by large-breasted women who wish to reduce the appearance of their breasts by a cup size or two.

God knows there are times where we need discretionary people in our lives, people who know how to calm things down and defuse the obvious. When you are overendowed or well endowed, sometimes you need people who know how to turn it down a notch. It's funny, but as I write this to you, there is a common colloquialism on reality TV called "turned up." It's used to describe how this generation acts when things are super hyper or loud or about to jump off or bust out, but thank God for minimizers. These are the people who let you know that things, obstacles, problems, and storms aren't as overwhelmingly big as they appear. They can come along and show you the bite-sized benefits of not "turned up," but being turned down works just as well.

Maximizer/push-up bra: these bras lift the breasts and emphasize cleavage through their unique structure and extra padding. The padding may come in various forms, such as water sacks or silicone inserts. The goal is to give a fuller, more natural look to breasts of all sizes.

Did I say, "Who let the girls out?" Well, call Shug Avery, honey, because we are on our way to Memphis (a line from one of my favorite movies— The Color Purple). Listen, you have to have at least one maximizer-bra person in your life. This is the person you want to come and let it all hang out. Now this person may be the eclectic of the crowd—the voyeur of sorts. Or maybe this person is the wild child that no one but God will one day tame, but they help you get the attention you want and don't want. Let me explain—as I said in an earlier chapter, men are visual, so they just assume you are willing to share what you are willing to show. My only advice is to proceed with caution, because, I tell you, these people do everything on Front and Main Streets. As they used to say where I'm from down souf ("south"—work with me—you know I'm kuntry), they "ain't got no shame in their game" but still, all things work together for the good. These people help you get out of your shy box and show you how to have great "curb appeal," as they say in real estate, but make sure you are ready to sell the house before you list it on the market. If you put some bait in the water, you might catch a fish, but some fish you have to throw back because they aren't ready yet.

> Sports bra: sports bras are made for active women who engage in rigorous physical exercise. They are designed to be comfortable and supportive by holding the breasts in place during motion; therefore, reducing damage to soft tissues of the chest. These bras are usually made of stretchable material to provide a snug fit.

Last but not least, there are the sports bra like people. When I was in high school (I'm dating myself like an old refrigerator—I can't hold nothing), there was a music icon named Cindy Lauper. She released a song called "Girls Just Want to Have Fun." It became an instant hit. Well, those of you who remember the video—it showed girls doing everything from playing rough sports to mowing the lawn—nothing supple and soft but rugged and rowdy. It showed a liberation of sorts for women who were normally seemingly held down in a male-dominated world. You need sports-bra people for the rugged moments in life. When times get turbulent and you get hit with unexpected bad news or are going through relationship challenges with your spouse or a separation, you know they've got a spare bedroom; or during divorce, they keep the kids for you. These are the people that help you hold things in place. They are built for the times when you need protection so you won't get damaged.

Affirmers

I love words because words allow us to express truth to power. We all need affirmer-bra people in our lives who allow us to shine without shame.

Definition of affirmation

af·fir·ma·tion [àff r máysh'n]

1.   act of affirming: an assertion of support or agreement

2. something affirmed: a positive statement or declaration of the truth or existence of something

Yes there are some things in life that are true whether we choose to accept them or not—ignore them, or just wish they were not so. This includes everything from postpartum to the need for surgery because medicine and radiation and chemotherapy were no longer the option. Then there is the lighter side—there is help in place to make things easier to manage. These are what I call affirmation-bra people, and they serve the most important roles of all. They are there for every single stage and phase to cover, comfort, and conveniently aid us through the vicissitudes of life. These are the people who understand that just because things don't work out the way we plan, it doesn't mean they can't still work out. These are the people who affirm us wherever we are on life's journey. They understand that a bend in the road ain't the end of the road, and from their experience, we draw strength. Bishop T. D. Jakes, one of my mentors, told the story of how his mother, before transitioning on to be with the Lord, once had to have a very sensitive surgery. He noted the obvious differences between the day nurse and the night nurse. He said that the morning nurse was short and mean and sometimes unaccommodating to his ailing mother, who had just come from under the knife, yet the night nurse was sweet and sensitive and very obviously went the extra mile to make sure that Mrs. Jakes was comfortable. After watching this behavior, he asked the night nurse what the difference was between her and the day nurse because they both had very different bedside manners. Was it the schooling or the medical training? The night nurse responded that she treated his mother with that kind of care not only because it was her job but because she had had the same surgery and knew the pain it caused. Having said that, affirmers let us know that we can make it because they've been through similar and survived, and they also let us know that we don't have to be ashamed—from the boardroom to the bedroom—from the delivery room to the recovery room.

> Built-in bra: a built-in bra is one that comes with the clothing—eliminating the need for a separate bra. This style can be found attached to the insides of swimsuits and tube tops. Some built-in bras are just horizontal, elastic fabric, but others have padding and underwired cups, as well.

You need some built-in bra people who are with you and along for the ride. They are insiders. They mostly can get wet or get put. The joy of them is that they don't require any effort because no matter what, they are always there.

> Shelf bra: this bra covers only the lower part of the breasts, leaving the nipples and upper part of the breasts exposed. It is not supportive and is worn in sexual situations.

Nakedness is sometimes awkward, yet, we are born this way; and in other countries, it is a norm. Because of a perverted society, nakedness is shunned. But a shelf-bra person is there to let you see life through the lens of half-empty and half-full. They understand how to get out of the way, make the announcement, and sit back down. These are your low-maintenance people.

> Peephole bra: a peephole bra features holes around the nipples. Its loose coverage of the entire breasts is insufficient to provide significant support. This type of bra is also worn in sexual situations.

These are the private people who get access-only credentials. They are allowed into certain areas that are off-limits to others. They serve a certain purpose—these are event people. Allow me to explain; there are 3 seasons of people in your life. There are the people who are in your life for an event, those who are there for an era, and those who are there for an eternity. The problem is many of us suffer from separation anxiety and we normally hold people beyond their appointed time, so please note that peephole bra people are only there for an event; not for an era nor an eternity. One of the worse things you can do is try to turn event and era people into eternity people. Please don't confuse them.

> Maternity bra: women's breasts become more sensitive, heavier, and larger throughout pregnancy. Maternity bras are adjustable and can expand to take these changes into account.

Maternity-bra people are affirmers of the era of giving birth on through breast-feeding. They understand that your body has gone through certain changes and challenges, and the need for comfort and convenience are of the utmost importance. These people know that you are uncomfortable because of what you carry, so they are there to take the load off and make it easier to endure. These people are not easily offended.

Nursing bra: these bras are worn to ease the breast-feeding process. They are made with flaps that can be unclasped or pushed to the side, keeping the breasts supported during breast-feeding.

Now, these people know one thing—it's all about accessibility. They prevent total exposure, yet they affirm the fact that there is a need. They may have to be pushed aside or unclasped because there is a greater need. Again, they know that milk and nourishment and feeding are a must, and they aid and assist during the process. They know how to keep it moving and are not easily embarrassed. Also note that these are people who are not overly sensitive and they refuse to walk around wearing their feelings on their sleeves.

Mastectomy bra: a mastectomy bra is intended for women who have undergone the removal of one or both breasts due to cancer treatments. Here, the cups are made with pockets to keep breast prostheses in place and simulate the existence of breasts.

Listen, this is the most important bra of all, because, my sista, I want to affirm that just because there was an issue with your tissue that your organs can still be ornaments. These bras are the people that bring a sense of normality when life has thrown us a curveball or two. These are the people that cover us in class and don't shine light as to shame. Cancer: I serve notice that you may have slowed us down, but you ain't stopped nothing. This goes out as a clarion call to all my sistas who have endured this dreaded disease. I decree and declare that you are still women, and those of us who are mastectomy-bra people affirm that you are still in the game. You remind us that good-bye don't mean gone. Love ya to life!

Choosing a suitable bra is indeed a challenge these days. One bra does not fit all; range of activities. For instance, a regular jogger should purchase a good sports bra, while a more social woman should spend on convertible bras that fit her many formal evening outfits. Whatever whatever the case, I warned you this was going to take a while, but we made it. And for all of you who must have some retail therapy in order to survive, well, you got it in.

There is nothing like having the right bra for the right moment!

CHAPTER 12

Who Let the Girls Out?
Can You Fasten Me Up? Here Is Some Help with Your Hooks.

This has been a fascinating journey, but now that you know your CUP size and we've gone BRA shopping, let's hook the bra. Your life is waiting on you to walk the red carpet, so you don't want to be late.

I have homework for you as you prepare to live out loud. By all means, be authentic.

au·then·tic *adjective* \ - **then-tik, o-** \ : real or genuine : not copied or false

: true and accurate: made to be or look just like an original.

Those who remember the '80s, remember the soft drink wars between the two soft drink kingpins, Coca-Cola and Pepsi-Cola. I remember the taste-test commercials where they would put a representative of the product in a mall or on a busy street and they would ask complete strangers to do a blindfolded taste test. They would have an off-brand cup of soda and the actual soft drink, and the person blindfolded had the arduous task of telling without looking which one was the real thing or not. Come to think of it, Coca-Cola's campaign slogan was "Can't beat the real thing" and Pepsi's was "You got the right one, baby."

Nonetheless, the contest was something that we can apply to our everyday lives. Can people testify to your authenticity while blindfolded; or, once tasting your presence—could they say that you are not who you say you are?

News flash: *by all means, be you!* Not your image, not your job, or your career, but be you. Be your CUP size. Be authentic.

Here Is a Clue

In life, we spend most of our time getting, having, or doing. We are either getting something, we are busy trying to have something, or we are overly occupied by doing something, and it becomes a cycle of getting, having, doing. But the truth of the matter is this—you were not created to be a human getting, having, or doing. You were created to be a *human being*. When was the last time you just made time *to be*? Be human, be normal, be content, be patient, be prudent—no deadlines to meet, no egos to stroke, no butts to be kissed, no airs to put on, no bosses to bow to. Just breathe and *be*. Be a human being. Authenticity is being real. It's not about what you have on, but rather it's about what you have in. There's no need to scam or be slick or play mind games or manipulate. Just be. Dave Ramsey said it best "we buy things we don't need with money we don't have to impress people we don't like."

Then, once you've mastered the art of being and checked out of the rat race, the next step is to get out of the blame game and let go of your story. Whether you want to believe it or not, you, my friend, have developed a story about your life. We learn in story form even from the earliest of our existence. We've been taught by parables—Humpty Dumpty sat on a wall, Humpty Dumpty had a great fall, all the kings horses and all the kings men couldn't put Humpty Dumpty back together again. Three little pigs. Little Miss Muffet sat on a tuffet, eating her curds and whey. Little Red Riding Hood. Jack and Jill went up the hill to fetch a pail of water, Jack fell down and broke his crown, and Jill came tumbling after. Stories have played a big part in the shaping of our culture. However, we make up our own stories as a way to excuse the way we are.

For instance, we say stuff like, "My father was abusive, and my mother was never there, and I had to take care of myself, so that's why I am standoff-ish." Or well say, "If you knew what happened to me when I was seven, you would understand why I don't trust people." Or, "Well, my parents were alcoholics, so I don't socialize because people are not who you think they are." Or, "My first spouse cheated on me, so that's why I don't have any friends." Whatever your story is, it is very evident that once we try to get to know you that you are sticking to it and you have very much bought into it because you've been in your story for so long that you wear it like a badge of honor, and all we have to do is talk to you for ten minutes, and it starts to leak out.

Then there is the other problem—the blame game. We love to play the blame game. And we get it from our ancestors, Adam and Eve. You remember when God left Adam in charge of creation and Eve was beguiled by the serpent, and they ate of the tree with the forbidden fruit? When God came back and saw that their world had been rocked, God asked Adam what happened. Adam blamed Eve, for he said, "That woman you gave me." And then God asked Eve why she did what she had done, and she said, "It was the serpent's fault." So it was Blame Game 101 and no one wanted to take responsibility. My point for saying this is that we love to place blame on others in our past or life experiences because we get to make them into monsters. It's much easier to blame momma and daddy or your third-grade teacher because that means we can hold someone accountable for our issues.

Now, don't get me wrong. I'm not saying that there are not plenty of people out there who have been raped, molested, abused, and suffered some trauma that may be suffering long-lasting effects on or are causing some behaviors. If that's the case, get some counseling and refuse to allow the enemy to make you stay there in that dark place and constantly relive it.

Refusing to let go of the story and continuing to blame others just so you have the feeling of justifying behavior patterns is not the answer, the whole point of knowing your CUP size is so that you can finally have the freedom to live and soar at the next level; however, if you are refusing to let go of your story, then go back and reread this book ASAP.

The *Real* on Keeping it Real

There is such a need to be accepted that we sometimes compromise our identities daily for acceptance by people who really don't love us authentically. We become accustomed to conforming to the moment until we lose out on the truth because we've lived this lie so long that it has become our truth. Living a lie is just as bad as telling one, so in this race to be wanted and accepted, we become products of our environment, which makes us, on one front, a pawn for the merchant who pushes and peddles his wares by placing his garments on the right star, so now because the popular star of the moment has it, we all have to have it.

The other extreme which deals with the pressure of what I call *Keeping Up with the Kardashians* syndrome, is we lose ourselves chasing a lifestyle we saw on a reality TV show. News alert! That's not *your reality*, In many cases, it's really not theirs, either. It was a cheap trick, because fads and fashions depend on a trend that says when you're hot, you're hot, and when you're not, tweak it and make it hot.

It drives societies' average Joes and Janes to steal, lie, cheat, and even kill to fit into social statuses that, at the end of the day, don't matter. We buy clothes that don't look good on us or aren't even made in our size. We get hairstyles that look good on other people. Why? Because that's our ideology of acceptability. It's what breeds jealousy, envy, covetousness, and contempt because we all want what looks good in a bad way. Someone once said he who dies with the most toys wins, but my question is, if you're dead, how do you know you won? It's this illusion of bad that drowns out good. Good finishes last, and good girls don't look as cute or get the man becomes the deception in people's minds! So doing good seems worthless; but as the writer of Psalms 37 says, do good and dwell for evermore.

27 Depart from evil, and do good; and dwell for evermore.

28 For the LORD loveth judgment, and forsaketh not his saints; they are preserved for ever: but the seed of the wicked shall be cut off.

Psalm 37:27–28 (KJV)

This text declares right always wins.

Dwelling has to do with security and longevity. Evil at its best, the writer mentions all throughout the passage, is only temporal. It doesn't last. The writer of Psalm 37, says stuff like, "The wicked sprang forth like a green bay tree and were no more," meaning they were overnight successes who were really one-hit wonders parading in the light but fleeing just as fast. They had no sticking and staying power. I remember as a kid a television character named Baretta used to say, "Crime doesn't pay." So if you do the crime, be ready to do the time. The writer understood this because he had lived long enough to see the end of the wicked. I trust him because they did their dirt and were dead, and he was left to tell about it. He says they were good starters but weren't finishers, and the sad reality is; when doing evil, it's not a great career move because its chews you up and spits you out before you know it, and you go from being the hottest at first to being the coldest, almost overnight. The fast life, they call it—fast in the fact that it's not forgiving, but it's just a sad carbon copy of nothingness camouflaged in something's clothes. It has no real identity. I'm reminded of one of my daughters who pressed me one day to buy her a bottle of bubbles, and so upon the purchase, we arrived home, and she leaped from the car and ran into the yard and pulled out the stem and started blowing bubbles. They were beautiful and almost seemed magical, but after blowing the bubbles, she would chase them. As soon as she would grab the bubbles, the bubbles would disappear in her hands. Well, she grew rather tired, as chasing bubbles soon got old. That's the way inauthenticity is. When chasing it, it's like chasing bubbles, and when you catch it, it's empty and disappears, leaving you with nothing. My question is—how long are you going to chase bubbles?

It is the same ways for us with the bubbles we chase! The drugs chasing the first high, the alcohol chasing the first buzz, the sex chasing that first orgasm—they're all a utopia that dissolves into a life ending in an unmarked grave with the epitaph that reads "Born ? — Died ?" Between the numbers lies a dash because all you did was live in the dash.

So let's look at the benefits of good. The author says, "Do good, and dwell," which is an incentive. Have you noticed that evil only breeds temporal satisfaction and that it's short-lived, but the people who led you to it can't be found? Therefore this makes us observe the company you keep, because where you dwell is not as important as who you dwell with.

Your companions can make you or break you. They either inspire and encourage you to be better or they enlist you into evil and take you down in their sinister plots.

I love *The First 48*. Why, you ask? Because I feel like a shade-tree detective. The part I hate about the show is when young people who were just along for the ride end up getting sentenced to the same thirty-year, forty-year, fifty-year, or life sentences as the perpetrators of the actual crime. They were guilty by association, and now, more lives are lost just because of a crowd that chose not to do good.

The dwelling also has to do with company as well as consistency. Yes, practice makes perfect. The writer says that if you want staying power and if you do good long enough, it will become habitual and second nature. It's a progression because at first you are coached into it, and then it becomes your norm, but it's a change, which means that your initial departure from evil—although a choice—was done through coercion. Now that you consistently do good, it is a result of your conversion. One has to do with outer and the other with inner.

One day, when I was a child, my father went to purchase a van one day. After being hosted and hounded by this particular salesman, we happened upon two vans—same make, year, model, and color—but there was one difference: price. We asked about the difference in price because they looked the same. The salesman replied that the other one cost more because it was a conversion van. We asked, "Well, how can that be? They both look the same."

He said, "You won't be able to tell the difference until you get inside." We got in, and the conversion van had amenities like rear air-carriage seats and a list of little bells and whistles that the first van lacked. What made the difference? The inside. It was an inside job. So that's why we should do good. The more you do it, the more change takes place on the inside.

That other life wears out your body, and the collateral damage of the mental fallout is catastrophic. You look old before your time. Your physical capacities are well worn out from the years of multiple partners who gave you their beds but not their names. The hangovers and drug binges have fried your brain cells, and so it leaves you with bad lungs, bad liver, a bad life that is cut short. Now don't get me wrong, with good it's no insurance against sickness or tragedy, for God is no respecter of persons and He is also a just God; he rains on the just as well as the unjust. It's rather the assurance, because if you noticed the wicked were left by their so-called friends, but the good were comforted by their friend in Jesus.

This leads lastly in this section to the power of partnership again. The world grasped this idea and ran with it. Partnerships go on all around us—partnerships like Taco Bell and Pizza Hut; KFC and Long John Silver's; Wendy's and Tim Horton's. I mean, all the time these mergers go on right under our noses, yet, we fail to catch the vision on that concept, refusing to partner altogether or partnering with the wrong people. Begin to reevaluate the partnerships and relationships by asking the following questions:

1. Does this person or group of persons add value to my quality of life?

2. Do I add value to their lives?

3. Do we accomplish anything positive while in each other's presence?

4. Do we share destiny, or are we just so used to being around each other that we don't want to own the fact that our season may be up?

5. Lastly, am I better because of them, or do they rob me of my investment and don't reciprocate, making the relationship one sided?

In conclusion, the other benefit of doing good is longevity. The word *evermore* is not as much about remaining as much as it is preparing for the eternal. When the body dies, the soul has to move. How you live here determines where you will live later because Heaven is a prepared place for prepared people, but if you put an unprepared people in a prepared place, it won't be long before the place starts looking like the people. Why would you want to do evil all your life and expect to go to a place designed for those who do good? Well, that's the point. God doesn't expect for us to be sinless; he expects for us to grow and sin *less*. That's right. The ideology is in your walk with God. He warns in this psalm, "Don't drink the Kool-Aid." Wickedness doesn't pay, but when you commit to doing good, he walks alongside you. You then have "Emmanuel" it means God with us.

Psalm 23 states, "Yea, though I walk through the valleys of the shadow of death." Shadows won't hurt you, but they will make you hurt yourself. Shadows are signs that the real thing is close by. It's not death but a shadow of death. Before, you could run up the stairs and not miss a beat, and now you get tired walking down the stairs. That's a shadow of death. When you go in a room and forget what you went there for, that's a shadow of death. Looking for your glasses and they are on your face; picking up the phone and forgetting who you were going to call; looking for your keys and they are in your hand, that's the shadow of death. When you comb your hair and there's more hair in the comb than on your head, I'm sure you get the picture. Well, the truth is, where will you spend eternity? There is only one guarantee: surrender your life. Doing good doesn't mean you are in charge; it means you've been changed. But here is the promise. He says, "Thou art with me." "Thou is Parakletous" means to come alongside to help. He comes alongside of us to help us. We need the Paraclete. You may say, "Well, I'm not familiar with 'Paraclete,' but I am familiar with 'paraphrase.'" A paraphrase is another way of saying the same thing. For instance, if I can't say, "Jehovah jireh, Jehovah tsidkenu, Jehovah shaloam, Jehovah rophi," I can say, "Bridge over trouble water, leaning post in a time of trouble, friend in a lonely hour, shelter in a time of storm." It's just another way of saying the same thing. Well, you may have never heard Paraclete or paraphrase, but maybe you've have heard of paragon. A paragon is when one superior comes face to face with another superior. For instance, for every name I call in the human race, there is another name to meet its match. If I say George Washington, I can say Abraham Lincoln. If I say Muhammad Ali, I can say Mike Tyson. If I say Michael Jordan, I can say LeBron James. If I say Mickey Mantle, I can say Sammy Sosa. But when I say Jesus, the human race has to close its mouth.

You've never heard of Paraclete, paraphrase, or paragon, but maybe you are familiar with parasol. A parasol is an umbrella that covers you when it rains. Well, that's just like Jesus. He doesn't always stop it from raining, but he shelters in a time of storm. Maybe you are not familiar with Paraclete, paraphrase, paragon, or parasol, but maybe you are familiar with parachute. Parachutes normally are for falling. Well, that's just like Jesus. He won't always stop you from falling, but He will let you down easily.

Maybe you've never heard of Paraclete, paraphrase, paragon, parasol, or parachute, but you have heard of paramedic. A paramedic is not like a regular doctor because normally when a person gets sick, they have to go see the doctor, but with the paramedic, the doctor comes to see you. Well, that's the way God is. When you can't get to church and your pastor is not around, you have a doctor in Jesus who will come see about you. If you are not familiar with Paraclete, paragon, paraphrase, parasol, parachute, or paramedic, one day we are going to a place called Paradise, but the only thing that guarantees it is if Christ is your companion, and with Him, you don't have to fear evil. Do good and dwell forevermore.

Follow the Plan

> [11] For I know the thoughts that I think toward you, saith the LORD, thoughts of peace, and not of evil, to give you an expected end.

—Jeremiah 29:11 (KJV)

> [11] I know what I'm doing. I have it all planned out—plans to take care of you, not abandon you, plans to give you the future you hope for.

—Jeremiah 29:11 (MSG)

Plans are so important. Wherever you live right now, whether you live in a palace or an apartment, it was built by a contractor or construction company who had to follow a set of plans, or blueprints. God has a divine plan and blueprint for your life and sometimes it may not make any sense. I remember so vividly that at a church I used to pastor; we did a renovation project of almost a million dollars on the educational wing. When they first started, there was a lot of tearing up, so much so that I wondered in the early stages if we had hired the wrong contractor. Meanwhile I learned one of the biggest lessons I've ever learned in my life, and that was before you can properly renovate something, there must first be some demolition. Things have to be torn out and thrown out, because if not, you will put new stuff on broken junk, and they won't match, and you will end up with a great big ol' mess. Soon after that process, things began to take shape, and that was awesome. I got a chance for the first time in my life to see an elevator built and installed from start to finish. I remember so vividly I felt like a kid the day that the ThyssenKrupp elevator people showed up (ThyssenKrupp is the top elevator company in the world), and I had to have an elevator installed because the seniors couldn't take climbing all those stairs to get up to the sanctuary without having to climb several flights of stairs and I wanted the best. The day they arrived, I asked like a kid in a candy store if they minded if I safely watched them do it, and they agreed. And the first thing they had to do was to come in and dig a seventy-yard hole straight down for the piston to go up. I was blown away. Anyway, forgive me for my nostalgic moment on memory lane, but I noticed something else on our construction site—every one of the subcontractors who came in to work on the building requested a copy of the plans, from the plumbers to the electricians. They all worked from the architect's blueprints. Well, girlfriend, if you are going to maximize, you've got to do it according to the master's plans.

Now I know some of you are probably saying, "Well, I thought you told us we need to have a plan." Yes, you do, but in knowing your CUP size, you understand from the outset that your plans should line up with His plans, because I guarantee that even when things look torn up and are a mess, if you stick to the plan, you will be more than satisfied with the end result and the finished product. Let's look for a moment at what Jeremiah said.

What's interesting about this particular passage that I hear quoted so many times is that when it was written, the children of God were in seemingly a bad predicament. They were in bondage and captivity for seventy years. Seven is God's number of perfection, and ten is God's number of judgment, so they were in perfect judgment. But when the judge of judges is on the case, you don't have to worry. He knows how to be fair with His sentencing, because at this point in Jeremiah chapter 29 God people were in this captivity all because they failed to follow God's law of allowing the land to rest every seven years; it was called the year of jubilee. It's when in the Mosaic days every seven years people would forgive debts owed and grant freedom to those who were slaves or servants. It was a time of release, renewal, refreshment, resetting and, yes, rest. But the children of Israel ignored the fact that even the land deserved a break, because it had worked hard to produce for seven years straight. Imagine working seven years straight without a day off. So in order to give the land a reprise God placed them in bondage, where they were carried away from their land and forced to give the land rest. God was telling them through the prophet Jeremiah that in spite of some stuff, God still had a plan for them.

Aren't you glad we serve an "in spite of" God? That even when He has to chastise me, He still has me on His mind? He never abandoned us to a permanent time-out or made us go stand in some eternal corner, but yet, he is a God who loves us through it and in it in spite of.

You see, we live in a society where we have raised a generation that feels there should be no consequence or punishment for bad or ill behavior, even on television when high-profile people like stars and the powerful, popular, wealthy people who have money are convicted of crimes. It's almost expected that they will just get a slap on the wrist. Now the legal system will allow a cocaine cartel kingpin to buy his way out of trouble because he can afford high-powered attorneys, and then the average poor person gets twenty-five years for the same thing that a star got probation and a suspended sentence for. Anyway, that's for another book, but God is just and not fair. If He were fair, He would have had to kill us every time we sinned. "Sin" in its original language is "harmetia," which means "to miss the mark." The Bible says the wages or penalty or payment or retribution is death. That's fair, but God looks beyond our faults and says, "Where sin abounds, my grace abounds more." In other words, whatever the sin, God's got some grace that will cover it cure it or cancel it.

So God says to his people, "My plans for you are to bring you out of this bondage, and after the seventy years, I have an expected end—a potent and positive and powerful future for you." Now, I know you are probably saying, "What? I don't have seventy years to wait on my deliverance." No, what I'm saying is that we are under grace now, but we can learn a lesson or two or three from people who were shown grace even while under the Law.

He says to them that His plans for them had nothing to do with three things:

Number one, His plans had nothing to do with *people* who they were exposed to. Now so that you can be clear, please understand that's not to say that God won't use people to bless you. As a matter of fact, Luke 6:38 says, "Give and it shall be given unto you; pressed down, shaken together, and running over shall *men* give unto your bosom." So, yes, God uses people, but our blessing and His mind toward us does not change because of people. He says to them, in essence, "My plans for you have nothing to do with people, namely, in this case, the Babylonians," who were their oppressors, their enemies.

Allow me to say—sometimes we give people too much power and credit, especially our enemies. These were only Babylonians. We must stop giving away our personal power to people who appear to have the upper hand. God says, "Stop telling me how big your problems are, and start telling your problems how big your God is." People are not *the* source they are just a *re*source. God is *the source*. So He says to His people, "My plans for you have nothing to do with the people around you," as if to say, "They can't stop, block, plot, scheme, or change my will for you." It doesn't matter, girlfriend, who doesn't like you. If your boss or supervisor or department head has it in for you, God says, "Don't let the people around you affect the person inside of you, for greater is he that is with in me than he that is in the world." You know your CUP size, and people can't steal that. You have *favor* from the Father.

Second, He says, "My plan has nothing to do with the ***present place*** you are enveloped by." Understand this, they were in bondage. What a horrible predicament. Yet in a foreign land, God had favor for His flock. They were in a place that seemingly was bad. But this is what He told them to do. Build some houses. Don't wallow in self-pity and feel sorry for yourselves. Build you some houses; don't let your surroundings suffocate your self-esteem. Build you a house. I give you real estate in your present state. Listen, it's not in the land, it's in the man. You've got to be so resolute about your CUP size, my sister, until you can build a kingdom in enemy territory. You are so valuable to God that even your enemies can't stop His favor. Even if they steal your stuff, they can't steal you favor. You have what it takes to build even in a bad place. Listen, if you do nothing else, stop cursing the ground where you stand. Stop looking at where you are, and start living where you are. You don't have to relocate because if you are running from yourself, you are still going to be who you are when you get to where you are going. God is not bound by geography. It can happen for you even where you are. Your present ZIP code does not dictate God's ability to move in your life. I dare you to prosper where you are. But He's not through because also in that present place He said to get married— that means to partner, where you are. And then He said to have some children—that means procreate where you are. All I'm trying to say is God's plans have nothing also to do with your present place.

Third, He said, "My plans have nothing to do with the people, your present place, but also it has nothing to do with your ***past experiences***." You see, they were there because of their past, but God says, "I'm not going to stop because you want to get stuck in stuff that happened in yesteryear." God says, "Live in spite of the past." He says to them, "Stop looking back. It's just because you've run into a situation." It's almost like when the children of Israel had left the flesh pots of Egypt, the Bible says they got to the Red Sea and wanted to kill Moses. Now, whether you are a biblical student or not, you've got to understand that when He delivered them out of Egypt, He used Moses as the deliveryman, and now that they are at the Red Sea, they are blaming Moses for their dilemma.

Allow me to say something, don't let what you see make you turn on your leader. Listen to what they said to Moses: "You've brought us out here to die. At least back in Egypt we had graves and decent burial grounds." *Are you kidding me?* They would have chosen a cemetery plot over freedom. They were looking behind them and driving with their focus on the rearview mirror. It's small for a reason. It was meant for glancing, not glaring and staring. Red seas are revealers of who's with you and who's not. Red seas reveal people's motives and thoughts. If you ever want to see who's really for you, just get to a red sea. God says to His people to stop looking in the rearview mirror and focus on the windshield—what's up ahead.

Last, God's plans have something to do with your ***perspective*** expectations. What's interesting to me is that God says to them in essence, "I have thoughts of peace and an expected favorable outcome." If you flip that "outcome" around, it says, "Come out." I want you to get the perspective of an expectant mother. Knowing your CUP size makes you fertile and pregnant, and I want you to focus on the delivery room. I don't have any spiritual epidurals. I just want to act as a spiritual **accoucheur (one who assist in birth)**, and I want to assist you into giving birth to your future. As a woman who knows her CUP size, "Eye hath not seen and ear hath not heard nor has it entered into the heart of man what God has in store for those who love him" (1 Corinthians 2:9). All I'm saying is change your perspective and live in expectancy. The baby is coming soon. Some changes gotta take place in how you dress, how you eat. Yes, you've been stretched, and stretching comes with stretch marks, but that's okay. What's in you will be all worth it when you deliver.

You Need a Coach (And Not the Purse)

I cannot express the need for coaching enough. I am going to make this— as they say where I'm from down south—cut-and-dry. We all need some coaching—not because its en vogue or chic, but because leaders are learners, and all activity is not productivity. You need to be coached in certain areas. Coaches cannot be on the field or the court with you, but they give you the tools to build your dreams and show you the possibilities of breaking your own records and plateaus and ceilings. Please understand your coaches are not your cheerleaders; they encourage and mentor us through our storms. Yes, you and I are going to have some miserable Mondays, some terrible Tuesdays, some wicked Wednesdays, some troublesome Thursdays, some frightening Fridays, some sorrowful Saturdays, and some somber Sundays. No need to cry because there is no exception to the rule. It comes at every stage and phase of this thing called life. You can be in your tender teens, your teachable twenties, your thrifty thirties, your forcible forties, feisty fifties, seasoned sixties, settled seventies, aching eighties, benevolent nineties, or your prodigious hundreds—trouble will come, however, wait because your end shall be peace. The Bible says where there is a multitude of counselors, there is much success.

You Need a New Coach

Okay, now that the past is dead, what's next? The grieving period, right? Wrong! We will not move forward crying over spilled milk. Now that we have departed, let's set our attentions on where we are headed, not where we left. You can't drive forward looking in the review mirror. That's why it's so much smaller than your windshield. Have you ever noticed that your windshield is huge and your rearview mirror is small? It's like that because your rearview mirror was made for glancing, not gazing. The windshield is what's in front; the rearview mirror allows you to glance at what's behind … and really, it's only good if you are trying to go in reverse.

Now it's time to get you a new coach.

Coach? Yes, coach. Michael Jordan, LeBron James, Maria Sharapova, Jackie Joyner-Kersee, Billie Jean King, Larry Bird, Babe Ruth, Venus Williams Tiger Woods… the list is insurmountable with names of great men and women athletes who played at the professional level. Yet we would've never known who any of these greats were had it not been for their coaches. Yes, I know they all were or are talented and gifted, and some even possess superhuman like qualities, but they had to be coached in order to be developed. You must understand that raw ingredients go in the cake, but knowing the recipe is what makes the cake. A lot of raw talent is out there, but being left uncoached will make you a somebody on the playground, but a nobody in other arenas.

Why do you need a coach? Well, you were coached in the wrong direction so many times in your old life. So in this new life, which is a cup sized life, you need coaching as well. Lets go back to Psalms 37:27-28 and finish what we started in the beginning of this chapter.

Departing from evil takes discipline but also direction. You must reprogram your mental hard drive if you want to live your life on purpose and with purpose. We discussed previously your choices which liberate you to looking through a lens of possibility, because it's hard to be optimistic with a misty optic. Therefore, you now have this newfound freedom, and you've gotten away from evil in the sense of the old environment and mind-set. You must now be coached toward an action plan, in which the writer gives us the key in the next clause, for he says, "Depart from evil." That sounds good, but what next? There it is: "Do good." What a conundrum David puts us in, as if we didn't have enough to deal with.

Do good. Wow. That sounds interesting because what good represented to me was to do what felt good, and the sad reality is everything that looks good ain't good. Money is good, if invested well. Friends are good if they can truly be trusted. Food is good if prepared in a healthy way and eaten in moderation. So, who and what determines the difference? Sex is good. As a matter of fact, God speaks benedictions on everything He made. Remember "Benediction" is a compound word that simply means good ("bene") words ("diction"). When God was in Creation mode, everything He made He said was good and very good, including and especially you and I, so this concept of good can be very expansive.

So how do I just do good? Well, I'm glad you asked. Let's have a quick English lesson. The author of this psalm says, "Depart from evil, and do good." The key is in the *and* portion. You see, *and* is a connecting conjunction, and so whatever is in front of *and* whenever you see it, it is connected to whatever is behind *and*. Therefore, there is a poignant pivot in the passage that suggests substitution, or replacing one thing with another. You must understand if you fill the voids with similar vices, then you've made no real progress, but when you replace with upgrades, the quality changes. One has to do with excavating and environment; the other has to do with enlisting and equipping with new energy. So let's connect the dots. You didn't stop dancing; you just changed partners. You need new coaching to adapt to the change because there is a major difference between little league and the pros. Here is the first lesson in being coached at the next level. If you spell *devil* and dropped the letter *d*, you have the word *evil*, and if you take the word *God* and add the letter *o*, you have the word *good*. Also one might consider that "evil" backward is "live" in order to live, you need to do the opposite of evil and the opposite of evil is good.

Here is the choice. You can deal with the devil and languish in evil, or you can pursue God and enjoy good. Let's cut a little deeper. You learned in the first phase you had to leave, because your environment can affect your condition and your position.

Watch this. I stated earlier that your nature causes you to gravitate toward things that you don't need. We do it all the time. What's not good for us, we tend to overindulge in; and things we need, we normally avoid—like the gym. Everybody wants to look good or lose weight, but no one wants to work out.

You need an environment that is conducive to your desired goals. It is a reality, sweetheart. Your environment will get in you or rub off on you. If you are in a room that's filled with smoke, you don't have to be a cigarette smoker, but the fact that you are in the room with smokers, the smell of smoke gets on your clothes, in your hair, and in your pores. Or if you are in a room full of marijuana smokers, you don't have to indulge, you can get high just by being there. Likewise, with this good and evil predicament. You must depart so it can no longer get on you or in you. That's the positional, now, let's deal with the conditional. We have choices. Now here is why coaching counts. Society programs you against your higher self-awareness or consciousness with entertainment and allurement. For example, let's look at promotions of products. It's the illusion in the entertainment that commercializes pleasure, but the end result is pain.

Basically, those who sell us amusing things make evil look good and market it so that you don't think and instead go against your God nature. For instance, they think we don't have dog sense. If you take some liquid and put it in a bowl and pour poison in it, a dog will walk up, smell it, and walk away from it because it refuses to drink poison. Well, they show us liquid poison all the time on the commercials. Alcohol says, "I will make you drunk and impair your judgement your judgment and cause you to harm yourself and others," yet, we go and purchase that poison. Not even a dog would do that.

Another example is cigarettes. The package says, "I may cause cancer," but people buy them and smoke them, knowing they could bring harm to them or their loved ones, but that's what we do. We gravitate toward the things that aren't good for us.

Coaching to do good—yes. We know by trade and training how to be evil. Now you need coaching in the opposite direction. A coach is called to take the unharnessed, natural, raw talent and redirect and package it into discipline and preparation that leads to success. Basically, coaching helps develop integrity and character. I learned this in the gym. I was attempting to lift some weight, but I didn't do the actual follow-through correctly. A man standing near said, "Let me spot you. I'm a coach." He was smaller than I was, so I thought, *Yeah, right. Him coach me?* Maybe he was just trying to showoff, but nonetheless I agreed, and he came and said, "trust me." He shifted me in order to shift the weight and supported me until I executed the movement properly. I never will forget the words he stated. He said, "I wanted to help you with that so you wouldn't hurt yourself." That blew my mind. He saved me a lot of pain and prevented possible injury by helping me do it right. Well, reality check. It's better to be a legend in your own time than in your own mind, and the bigger lesson is all activity is not productivity.

Getting proper coaching can spare you unnecessary pain and prevent life-threating injury.

Girlfriend, you need some help. Don't be an island. God has positioned people around you—some you know and some you don't—who can coach you into this arena of doing good.

God already declared that you were good when He made you, now it's time to be coached into that area. Stop trying to be Wonder Woman or She-Ra, and allow someone to coach you—be open, be teachable. Finally, there are two main reasons why you need coaching as you depart from evil. You can deceive yourself into thinking you are greater than you are and that you don't need anyone. But the Bible says where there is a multitude of counselors, there is much success.

There is an athlete who used to be in the NFL. He's not there anymore, but he was known as one of the greatest wide receivers the game has ever known, so much so, that when drafted, he signed to one of the biggest paydays in professional sports history. His name is Terrell ("T. O.") Owens. Well, his career was short lived. He was always blaming the quarterbacks for not throwing him the ball. He was extremely controversial in his private life and was regularly being dragged into court for a deluge of lawsuits that ranged from club shootings to paternity issues. Some thought this affected his ability to perform on the field because these legal issues were distracting, to say the least, but just as fast as his career took off, it came to an almost equally abrupt ending. He finally ended up being cut from the Seattle Seahawks in 2012. One owner said something so crushing in an interview when asked on ESPN after the news got out about why Mr. Owens was released, he said that it all boiled down to the fact that he was talented but not coachable. What a sad indictment on a six time Pro-Bowler. Don't let that be your testimony. In every arena, I hear of coaching—whether it's Tiger Woods in golf utilizing a swinging coach or Beyoncé bringing in a vocal coach. Think about it—if they need coaching to do good at their levels, and they are considered to be the best in their perspective fields, then what about us?

Lastly, you need coaching to depart from evil and do good because others can see what you can't see. I was in a Bible study one night, and a young lady commented on a point that I'd brought out, which was that we were living our lives—or rather, living *in* our lives—so we have a narrow scope from our own conclusions. She said, "Yes, Pastor, like you can't see your ears but I can." Confused by such an awkward statement, I asked her to explain. She said, "Well, you can't see your ears, but I'm looking right at them. You can see them if you go find a mirror, but I can see them because I'm looking right at them." I listened as she went on to explain, and she gave the analogy of when she used to go to clubs before she dedicated her life to Christ. One night she got as sharp as she could and put on an eye–catching, provocative outfit guaranteed to draw attention. On her way to the club, she stopped and got gas. She was so caught up in her own world that she wasn't paying attention. She got in a hurry, rushing to the club, and as she drove down the street, cars begin to honk at her and pull up beside her, blow their horns, and pointing in an attempt to get her attention. She was thinking they were harassing her, so she turned her music up to drown out the horns and put on her shades to ignore their obvious attempts. After all, she was dressed to kill and cleaner than a Thanksgiving chitterling. When she got to the club, she got out of the car only to discover the reason for their honking and pointing—her gas cap was hanging off and the gas tank door was open ... and she realized that she was inside the car, oblivious—they could see what she couldn't see.

Sometimes my beautiful queens, people can see things that we can't see. As a woman who now knows her CUP size, it is my hope that you walk in your Calling, embrace your Uniqueness, and lastly live out your Purpose.

Don't stop helping other women from 8-80 learn their CUP size. We have work to do and I won't stop until every woman on planet earth, regardless of color, or creed knows her CUP size.

Remember it's not about size it's about significance!

I LOVE YOU TO LIFE!

Get ready for the next level in My CUP Runneth Over! Coming SOON!

This is not "THE END" It's just an Intermission!

Charles Bond !

About Our C.U.P. Size Author

With a humble spirit that captures the hearts of listeners nationwide, Charles E. Bond, Jr. is reestablishing the simplicity of ministry. Literally becoming all things to all people, Bond is a pastor, teacher, motivational speaker, life coach, and singer; but it is his servanthood that has enabled him to impact the lives of men and women at all stages of life.

With the release of his first book, *"Every Woman Needs to Know Her C.U.P. Size (Calling, Uniqueness, and Purpose)*, Bond now adds another credit to his life and ministry—author! This powerful book addresses misconceptions women have concerning who they are as individuals, their relationships, and their ability to live life in fullness as God intended. Bond's sound Biblical principles, coupled with authentic life experiences, present a practical message that is empowering women to stand firm in their God-ordained purpose.

Known nationwide for his unique storytelling style of ministry, Bond has traveled across the country sharing a life-changing message in both word and song. With over 25 years of ministry experience, he has effectively served in Columbus, Ohio by addressing its financial and sociological needs, as well as spiritual. His strategic management of capital campaigns and formation of community partnerships have resulted in multi-million dollar community development projects within the inner-city. In March of 2013 God allowed him to Found and plant one of the fastest growing churches in the United States- New Wine Church International. Presently he is in the process of expanding that work as he and his parishioners prepare to launch a second location in March of 2015 to be located in the city of Memphis, Tennessee. New Wine Memphis shall be the name of the church.

Bond's work within the community is a testament that the truth and power of the Gospel he shares transcends the walls of local churches and reaches one soul at a time through a life that's lived amongst the people. In recent years, Bond was also voted the "Most Listened to Pastor" in Central Ohio and surrounding cities by an audience of over a quarter of a million listeners of his weekly radio program, *Help Us Lift Jesus*. With a synergy that bridges a hypnotic, southern style with the nuances of human condition, Bond freely shares a gift that elevates people above their circumstances. His passion inspires and leads audiences to a point of deliverance, whether he is sharing his heart one-on-one, preaching to a congregation, or impacting social media through nearly a million combined views on YouTube.

His vocal versatility has enabled Bond to share the power and love of Christ, bringing audiences out of despair and to a posture of hope. He has been privileged, yet humbled, to open up for some of the Gospel Greats such as Dorinda Clark, Vanessa Bell Armstrong, and Dr. Marvin Sapp. Magnetic in his persona yet humble in his heart, the richness and power of Charles Bond's vocal rendition of *Free at Last* leaves no listener unchanged. By intuitively connecting to unspoken emotions and the soul's longing, Bond's message provides a pathway for a meaningful encounter with God. The essence of his message mirrors our universal journey by offering us the best reflection of ourselves; the image that God intended all along.

Although he is many things to many people, Bond counts his highest office and achievement as being called *son* by a matchless God. As he works, he delivers a message of empowerment and victorious living. It is within such a work that his true purpose is truly fulfilled.

I Couldn't Forget about YOU!

This book would not be possible without some very special people. I dare not try to call every name for that would be another whole book within itself, because of the amazing cup-size people who have touched this anatomical cataclysmic ball of flesh called Charles Bond. I just wanted to take a minute and give you the unedited version of the people who although I am not a woman (nor do I desire to be) but keep in mind these are who I call my bra people.

Pastors Michael Benton, Nathan N. Nance , Kenny Turner(revin), Quinten L. Respress, Percy Winn, Joyce Meyer, Elder (Tamyra Tam Tam) Eddy where on Earth would I be without you?, my Columbus Crew- Pastors Rick and Michelle Reynolds.

Dr. R.A. Williams Jr. (WHW) and Dr. Kurtis (Sommy) Sommerville without you two, I am afraid of what America's pulpits would look like.

The people who have made my life easier include Pastors Mike and Lori Peterson who Pastor our New Wine Columbus Campus.

My daughter Brianna who is a CUP size Wonder. The world has not seen what God is going to do through you Bri. Your Balance is mind blowing and Daddy Loves you.

To the wonderful staff at Dogear Publishing who, I called so much and probably worried to death while stressing over this process. Thank you Dogear for your patience, I was a book writing virgin and you guys and gals allowed me to come into my own.

Last but not least to my new found friend and final editor Crystal Janine Olsen, thanks for not letting me put out a work that wasn't a proper representation of the excellence of my brand.

And the list goes on ……..if I didn't call your name here don't panic remind me before I RELEASE My Cup Runneth Over! Coming soon #CUPSIZEMATTERS # THISISJUST THE 1ST OF MANY